AF732256

PORSCHE
THE ROAD, SPORTS AND RACING CARS

DALTON WATSON
FINE BOOKS

PORSCHE - THE ROAD, SPORTS AND RACING CARS

First published in 1993

© 1993 Dalton Watson Fine Books

ISBN 1-85443-104-8

All rights reserved. Apart from any fair dealing for the purpose of private study, research, criticism or review, as permitted under the terms of the Copyright, Design and Patents Act of 1988, no part of this book may be reproduced or transmitted in any form or by any means, electronic, electrical, chemical, mechanical, optical including photo-copying, recording or by any other means placed in any information storage or retrieval system, without written permission from the publisher. All photographs are, wherever possible, credited to their source. Every effort has been made to ensure the accuracy of picture credits but if, for any reason, an illustration is not properly credited, or is not credited at all, the publisher apologises for any inconvenience caused and undertakes to correct such errors in future editions of this work.

British Library Cataloguing in Publication Data:-

Dalton Watson Team
Porsche cars
I–Porsche - The Road, Sports and Racing Cars
History
I–Title
629.2222

DALTON WATSON FINE BOOKS

Published by Dalton Watson Fine Books,
P.O. Box 2, Belton, Loughborough, Leicestershire LE12 9UW.
Printed and bound by Stamford Press Pte Limited, 48 Lorong 21, Singapore 1438.

PORSCHE - THE ROAD, SPORTS AND RACING CARS

PUBLISHERS PREFACE

This book was originally intended to be the work of two authors - both enthusiasts for the Porsche make of cars. However, time changed circumstances, with the result that four people have been the main contributors to the preparation of "Porsche - The Road, Sports and Racing Cars". Those four people have brought their own particular knowledge and skills to this work to make a team effort which we hope will be a source of great enjoyment to its readers.

Julian McNamara produced the outline manuscript for the book, then major contributions came from Mike Cotton and Jeremy Snook, both formerly Press and Public Relations Managers for Porsche Cars (Great Britain) Limited. Mike's acknowledged expertise in Porsche racing and rallying history complemented Jeremy's detailed knowledge of current production models. Chassis data came from Dr Ing hc F Porsche GMBH and from Porsche Cars (Great Britain) Limited, for which we must acknowledge the assistance of Jürgen Barth in Stuttgart and Angela Stacey at Reading. Dr David G Styles brought all this data together and tabulated it, as well as finally editing all the material brought together between these two covers.

Photographs have come from a wide range of sources. Many are from either the archives of Dr Ing hc F Porsche GMBH, Porsche Cars (Great Britain) Limited or their press outlets. Last minute pre-publication help came from Claire Titcombe in Porsche's Reading Press Office, whilst other pictures came from Rob de la Rive Box, Mike Valente and the authors. If any photographs are not properly acknowledged here, it is unintentional, for every effort has been made to verify the sources of all illustrations. Any oversights brought to the attention of the publisher will be recorded and rectified in any future editions of this title.

INTRODUCTION

Although this book is neither a biography of the family nor a history of the modern dynasty, some words on Dr Ing hc Ferdinand Porsche are well justified.

Born in Maffersdorf, in what was then Bohemia, on September 3rd 1875, Porsche was to find fame through an early fascination with electricity. In 1890 he drew local attention by wiring the family house for electric lighting. Later that year he took up an apprenticeship with Bela Eggar (later Brown Boveri) in Vienna.

The Weissach Development Centre, with hexagonal 'think tank' units, extended test facilities and a complete miniature race track.

Drawn towards the automobile, he patented a system of transmission by hub mounted electric motors in the later 1890s and left his job in the service department to join the old-established royal coachbuilding company of Lohner, as head of design.

By 1900 Lohner had built a front-wheel drive electric car using Porsche's system. The relationship lasted until 1905 by which time Porsche had drawn the company into heavy vehicles and the aircraft industry. His next move was to replace Paul Daimler, son of Gottlieb, at Austro-Daimler when Paul returned to Mercedes in Stuttgart.

The First World War saw the amalgamation of Austro-Daimler with Skoda. Porsche became head of design, demonstrating a flair for grasping the needs of the military and, by shrewd man-management, finding the people who could design workable means of meeting these needs.

In 1923 he followed Paul Daimler as technical director of Mercedes in Stuttgart, leaving his friend and protégé Karl Rabe in his place at Austro-Daimler.

Porsche's first task here was to revive the flagging reputation of the company in international competition. Out of this policy grew the fabulous SSK and SSKL sports cars and the following Grosser Mercedes. Also, not for the first time, he tried to interest his employers in a 'people's car'.

Thwarted in this, he accepted an offer made in 1927 by Steyr in Austria. The result was the magnificent Austria, the sensation of the 1929 Paris Salon. However, the Great Depression forced Steyr into amalgamation with Austro-Daimler, effectively squeezing Porsche out.

After considering an offer from the USSR to take control of its car industry, Porsche decided to branch out alone. Collecting a nucleus of talented people from his various past employers, he returned to Stuttgart.

His company 'Dr Ing hc Porsche KG' was entered in the commercial register on April 25th 1931. As his second in command he had recruited Karl Rabe, and Erwin Kommenda, a talented young engineer, joined from Mercedes Benz.

The formation by Audi, Horch, DKW and Wanderer, of the Auto-Union brought him work in the shape of the fabulous pre-war rear-engined Grand Prix cars. Even before this, however, the company had built up prototypes for Zündapp and NSU of a small rear-engined car heavily influenced by the Tatra company's 1933, Type 57.

By 1935 these cars led to the basis for the Volkswagen Beetle, a true 'people's car'. As early as 1938 Porsche was proposing a sports car based on Hitler's people's car. The end result was the VW Type 64 built for the Berlin–Rome race of 1939.

For the duration of the war the company was caught up in military projects. By 1944 they had been relocated to the picturesque town of Gmünd in Austria, to avoid Allied bombing.

It was from here, in 1945, that Porsche answered a call for consultation by Renault, gladly travelling into the French sector of Germany to help with the proposed R4. Unfortunately, while working on the project he was denounced as a war criminal by another French car maker. Arrested and imprisoned, both he and the company's assets were held to ransom by the French occupation forces.

Left in control of the company, his son, Ferry, began the construction of the limited series of Volkswagen-derived sports cars as a means of generating sufficient currency to free his father, and he accepted a contract from Piero Dusio to produce the Cisitalia 4-wd Grand Prix car. So began the modern history of the company.

Ferdinand Porsche was eventually released in 1947 but by this time his health had deteriorated. Having become an automotive legend in 75 years, he died in Stuttgart in January 1951 and was buried at Zell am See in Austria, the adopted family home.

THE FIRST PORSCHE CARS

In the summer of 1947 the first working drawings of what was to become the 356 were completed. Early in 1948 the first mid-engined 356 prototype took to the road, to be delivered by September of that year. The owner was a Mr R. von Senger of Zürich, one of the two original financial backers of the enterprise recruited by Ferry Porsche. By this time, with funds from Italian industrialist Piero Dusio and from the family estate, Ferry had managed to secure the release of his father and had regained the family's confiscated assets.

The first car (no. 001) was tested and demonstrated in April and May, and remained very much in the compass of the works, receiving its certificate of road-worthiness in Austria on June 8th. From the beginning it was used primarily as a research machine and, in keeping with the company's long-term policy of proving by competition, it won its first race in July 1948 at Innsbruck, driven by Herbert Kaes, a nephew of Ferdinand Porsche, and a development engineer with the company. The prototype was an open two-seater, unlike those that followed, and it was eventually delivered to von Senger when the need for his 7000 Swiss francs became imperative.

While the 001 had been built as an out-and-out sporting car, Ferry Porsche quickly realized that to produce such machinery exclusively would seriously limit the overall market available to the company. Further, the space frame was uneconomical to construct while the mid-engined layout meant a general lack of additional passenger and luggage space, as well as creating engine access problems. The solution to all these problems lay in adopting a project which Kommenda had originally instigated in 1946, a sleek coupé based upon a steel platform chassis, with the engine returned to the rear location, as in the Volkswagen Beetle.

For the proposed 1939 Berlin–Rome race Porsche designed and built an out-and-out sports racer on the VW floorplan. The cars bore the type number 64 and offered 40bhp. The resemblance to the later 356 can be clearly seen from these pictures. Of the three cars built, only one survives, in the hands of Austrian racing enthusiast Otto Mathé. It is pictured here at a historic racing meeting at the Nürburgring.

By the time the mid-engined car had received its certificate, the first two examples of this new design were complete. The steel floor pan carried torsion bar suspension and was stiffened by box sections at either side. The bodywork was in hand-wrought aluminium made by the nearby company of Weber. The first car completed was a coupé, the second a drop-head. Both received certification on August 7th and limited production was underway by November.

A month before this, in October 1948, Heinz Nordhoff had become chief executive at Volkswagen. He was shrewd enough to realize the potential of an on-going relationship between his company and the house of Porsche. The result was an agreement allowing Porsche access to Volkswagen parts on an OEM (Original Equipment Manufacturer) basis while retaining the consultancy services of Porsche's design bureau. Another benefit of this agreement was the opening to Porsche of the newly-inaugurated Volkswagen sales and services network, a godsend to the small, specialized and financially hard-pressed manufacturer.

Yet another step towards financial security came as Bernard Blanc, the second of the original Swiss financiers, secured space to exhibit a coupé and a drop-head at the 1949 Geneva Autoshow. The response was enough to bring about an important distribution deal with the AMAG group (already distributors for VW), which gave a cogent structure to servicing the vital Swiss market.

Sales and distribution thus assured, the next problem was to raise production to an acceptable level. For this the company needed to be back in the heart of the German automotive industry where both the local supplier's infrastructure and the freedom from restrictive Austrian import and export regulations would guarantee expansion.

Ideally, given both its general production requirements and the seriously impaired health of its founder, the company needed to return to its original location in Stuttgart. Unfortunately, the U.S. occupation forces had other ideas. They were occupying the old workshops and offices as a motor pool.

In the short term, compromises had to be made. Beutler of Switzerland became responsible for bodying some of the Gmünd cars, easing the pressure slightly, while Ferry negotiated an agreement whereby a limited homeward movement could be made by renting production space from the coachbuilders Reutters. The design and research staff were transferred back into temporary offices at the villa Ferdinand Porsche had built for himself in the 1920s. The first cars were ready for delivery in March 1950.

By this time Scania-Vabis had become distributors for Sweden, thereby opening the only other intact hard currency market in Europe. When Gmünd production finally halted on March 20th 1951, some 15 of the 46 production 356 Alu series had been accepted by the Swedish company – all of them cabriolets.

Of the production cars from Gmünd, the total was split into 23 coupés and 23 drop-heads, 18 of which were bodied by Beutler. Eight cars were assembled or built by Tatra in Vienna. One car was built by Kastenhofer. The factory retained five coupés for racing and research.

Sadly, Ferdinand Porsche died in January 1951, much weakened from his postwar imprisonment. Nonetheless, his staunch adherence to excellence in design and engineering was to become the cornerstone of the international rise of the company he had founded, and which he had nursed through some of the most difficult years of the century.

Ferdinand and Ferry Porsche beside the prototype 001 at Gmünd in 1948. The mid-engine layout was superseded by the rear positioning, but the overall styling established with this model was to last throughout the 356 production run.

Now part of the collection in the Porsche museum, prototype 001 is shown at the Nürburgring during celebrations marking the 50th anniversary of the founding of the company.

The steel-bodied 356

The steel-built 356 marked the beginning of the second phase in the Porsche saga. It was the car which brought them into international prominence as a quality manufacturer and marketing house, yet, because of its reliance upon Volkswagen components and its familial similarity in styling, it welded the image of the early sports cars firmly to the ubiquitous 'beetle'.

Production in Stuttgart built rapidly. On March 21st 1951 the 500th car was delivered – a situation contrived to coincide with the firm's début at the Le Mans 24-Hour Race. Of three aluminium cars entered – all with the original 1086cc engine to allow competition in the 1100cc class – only one survived the practice sessions. In the hands of Auguste Veuillet, the French importer, with co-driver Edmond Mouche, the car won its class, finishing 20th overall at an average of 122kph (76mph). The company thus had its first major international success, at the same time learning valuable lessons about racing preparation.

In the early years, the resemblance of the cars to their humbler Volkswagen cousins allowed the company to market a range of tuning accessories for Volkswagen. As well as providing the company with valuable mass-market turnover, this had the effect of offsetting some of the development cost on more prestigious projects. The first cars were little more than a 'beetle' engine and running gear beneath a smooth shell. Later cars were almost entirely originated at the Porsche factory.

From the very beginning there were some highly significant differences in the Stuttgart cars. The steel bodywork was the result of Reutters being unable to guarantee either quality or quantity when working in aluminium. The earliest 1086cc engines carried Porsche-designed alloy cylinder heads, while the 1288cc and 1488cc engines with which the company extended the range in 1951 for the 1952 model year, owed little more than the block to Volkswagen, and from 1952 the gearbox was totally Porsche-developed.

Such was the demand for the steel-bodied cars that, at an early date, cabriolet fabrication was seconded to the firm of Glaser. Certainly a main factor in this healthy early demand was the careful marketing of the cars – many were going to influential and famous personalities. It was a policy which was to continue over the years, adding immensely to the perceived glamour of the cars from Stuttgart. Another significant factor was the willingness of private owners to campaign the cars in competition; this in turn led to valuable feedback which was to play a vital rôle in the technological development of the company as a major racing manufacturer.

Chronology

1950–51

Steel-bodied coupé with split screen. 1086cc engine with alloy heads by Karl Schmidt of Neckarsulm. VW four-speed gearbox. Engine type 369, 40bhp at 4200rpm. Low bumper level.

1951

1300 introduced with Mahle chrome/alloy cylinders. 1286cc giving 44bhp at 4200rpm. 500th car built 21st March 1951, 1000th 28th August. 1500 with Hirth roller crank and Mahle cylinders type 502 (total production 527). 1488cc giving 60bhp at 4400rpm. Cabriolets built by Glaser. Bucket seats and rear bench standardized with front bench optional.

The Sauter Porsche was made by a Stuttgart businessman, Heinrich Sauter, to drawings prepared by Erwin Kommenda. The bodywork is lower than standard and has rear-hinged doors.

1952

1300 offered in 55bhp 'Dame' version. One-piece windscreen standardized and higher bumper line with deeper bodypanels. Alfinger crank adopted as alternative to Hirth roller crank on 1500 'Dame'-type 546 engine. Porsche synchro-mesh gearbox standardized. American Roadster introduced without wind-up windows and with divided windscreen, lightweight hood, and with 1500S engine giving 70bhp at 7000rpm (production no. 528). Total of 15 built to test U.S. market for the Speedster.

1953

1300S introduced with 589 engine giving 60bhp at 5500rpm from 1290cc 1300A with Alfinger crank introduced. Anti-roll bar added to front suspension.

1954

Type 540 Speedster introduced with choice of 1500A (546) or 1500S (528) engines. New three-section crank cases adopted. 1100 dropped in December.

1955–1959

356A introduced with rounded windscreen and many small modifications. Revised engines available were 1300 (506-2) 1290cc, 44bhp at 4400rpm; 1300S (589-2) 1290cc, 60bhp at 5500rpm; 1600 (616-1) 1582cc, 60bhp at 4500rpm; 1600S (616-2) 75bhp at 5000rpm. In addition to the Carrera, 1500GS, made its début using the 550 4-overhead cam shafts from the Spyder. Additional bonnet louvres and twin exhausts were the most visible distinguishing features. 15-inch wheels replaced the original 16-inch equipment over the range. In 1959 the D Type convertible replaced the Speedster. Bodies were by Drauz of Heilbronn. From 1957 all models had teardrop-shaped tail-light clusters. A 1600cc engine was used in the Carrera from 1958: the 1300 was discontinued late in 1958.

1959–1963

356B introduced at the Frankfurt Show, September 1959. Largely restyled with raised bumpers etc. D Type convertible production transferred from Drauz to d'Ieteren brothers in Brussels 1960. Removable hard-top available on normal convertible, hard-top coupé built by Karmann. Improved synchromesh on gearbox, renumbered Type 741. 1600S-90 (616-7) 90bhp at 5500rpm available from March 1960. In 1961 the range was face-lifted and the 1600S engine received cast-iron cylinders with four-ring, lead-coated pistons and a more efficient oil cooler, following revised con rods in 1960. Disc brakes arrived with the Carrera 2 in October 1961 along with a 2-litre 130bhp engine. Coupé and normal cabriolet built by Reutter.

1963–1965

356C, largely similar to post-1961 356Bs, was introduced in September 1963, featuring interior and external detail change. Disc brakes were fitted to all four wheels (ATE/Dunlop). The 1600S and S-90 were replaced by the 1600C (616-15) 1582cc, 75bhp at 5200 rpm and the 1600SC (616-16) 1582cc, 95bhp at 5800rpm. Gearbox modified from July 1963 to April 1965 (741C). The Carrera remained largely unaltered.

A Gmünd coupé, now a highly sought-after vehicle, pictured at the Pebble Beach *Concours d'Elegance* in 1982. The car is a 1949 model.

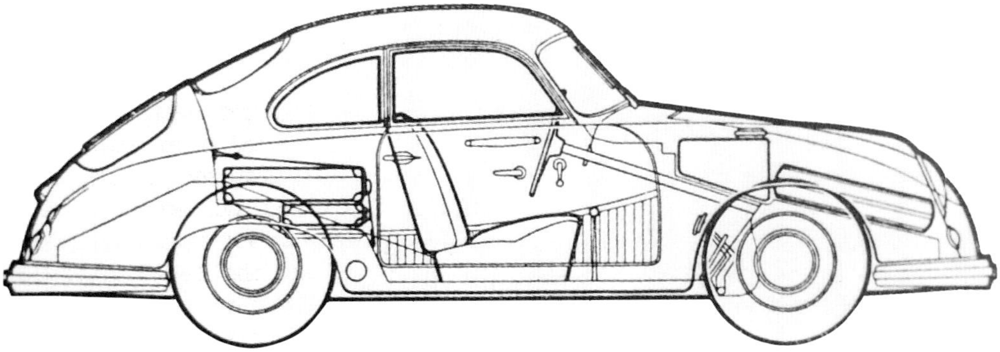

Two drawings of the 1950 Porsche coupé. Note the wrap-around bumpers and box sections

A 1950 Porsche on show in Geneva. Note the split windscreen and the Volkswagen wheels.

In 1952, the Porsche 356 received a one-piece windshield, V-shaped in the middle.

The 1957 356A with rounded windshield and small tail-lights. The luggage rack was optional.

The 356A had three round instruments. Of the 1600A Coupé a total of 7225 cars were built.

Engine capacities were raised to 1588cc in 1955, the 'Dame' version giving 60bhp (and a top speed of 100mph), the Super 75bhp and a top speed of 110mph.

In 1955 the Porsche 597 Hunting car was produced in small series, derived from the four-wheel-drive military vehicle produced in 1950, based on VW running gear of course.

The Speedster was the most exciting 356 derivative built and mainly intended for the American market. Only 4822 cars were built between 1954 and 1958.

A 1956 Porsche Speedster on exhibition at the Earls Court Motor Show. The British distributor was AFN Limited in Isleworth, then making Frazer-Nash sports cars and importing BMWs.

The Speedster is a popular car with repro-car makers. Certainly its soft profile would be hard to reproduce on a production line convertible of today.

A 1958 Speedster corners on the rugged edge on the *Course de Côte de Maune* (Belgium) September 1959.

The 1958 Carrera 1600, almost indistinguishable from the road Porsche 356A, though obviously much faster with its 4 overhead cam unit. The lowered suspensions, and extra cooling slots in the engine cover, are tell-tales for the 115bhp engine.

Inside, the 356 Carrera remains very functional, even with leather straps replacing window winders!

A 1963 356C Super 90 Convertible. This car was chassis number 157.803. Note the tear-drop shaped rear lights.

The successor to the Convertible D Type was the 356B Roadster, first built by Dannhauser, and then by the Belgian company d'leteren (as shown in these two pictures). It featured wind-up windows but no quarter lights.

Both the Porsche 356C-2000 GS and the Carrera 2 could be raced as well as employed for street use. This 1963 model developed 130bhp and was the quickest of all the production 356s, with a top speed of 125mph.

This 356C Cabriolet produced from 1963 to 1965 was the last fully convertible model made by Porsche until the 911 Cabriolet appeared in 1982.

The last model of the 356 was the C Type, built from 1963 until 1965. These cars had ATE disc brakes and slightly different ventilated pressed steel wheels.

Based on the 356B chassis, the 2000 GS-GT was a limited edition intended for competitions. At Sebring in 1963 the cars finished ninth and tenth overall and first and second in class. In the Targa Florio of the same year they finished third and fourth overall. Herbert Müller seen here in Schauinsland, became the 1963 European Hillclimb champion in one.

Carlo Abarth, an Austrian living and working in Italy, built 19 Carrera GTLs, first with 1600 and later with 2000 Carrera engines. The aluminium coachwork saved enough weight to keep the cars marginally competitive while the 904 was developed.

The Buchet/Aury Abarth GTL Carrera on the 1961
Tour de France.

The Porsche Abarth in a Swiss hill climb.

The 2-litre division was won by Ed Koch and Herbert Linge in a 356B Abarth.

Robert Buchet and Edgar Barth in a 356 Carrera Abarth in the Paris 1000kms, Montlhéry, in 1962.

THE 911 AND 959

If the 356 marked the emergence of the second generation of the Porsche dynasty, the 911 heralded the beginning of the third. Overall responsibility for the body development was once again the province of Erwin Kommenda but the styling was firmly under the control of Ferdinand Porsche III – 'Butzi'. Similarly, although development of the engine was in the hads of Hans Tomala, Ferdinand Piëch, a nephew of Ferdinand Porsche, was entrusted with detail design and the productoin. The specification was dictated by Ferry Porsche, who had instigated a programme as early as 1959.

Although announced as the 901 at the Frankfurt Show in 1963, it took one year to put the new model into production. By the time the car was launched the type number had been changed to 911, the result of a protest over zero numbers trade marks from Peugeot. In the interim period Porsche had acquired the bodybuilding assets of Reutter, the rest of the company being renamed Recaro.

With the launch of the 911, the company had a viable contender for the sector of the market which had previously been dominated by either expensive Italian exotica or specialist companies such as Aston Martin. Still, the original 911 displayed all the qualities of its successors. In keeping with the company policy the flat six was overhung at the rear and although weight had been saved by using the Biral aluminium-clad iron method of casting cylinders, the excess weight meant the car had a pronounced rear-weight bias, which in the short term was compensated by ballasting the front.

To increase luggage capacity, the front suspension was MacPherson strut while at the rear was Porsche's traditional transverse-torsion bar and trailing rear wishbone set-up. The brakes were the ATE discs used on the 356C. Dry-sump lubrication had been favoured at prototype stage for the 901 – a feature which was to be carried over into production. Another feature (but one to be dropped by the time of production) was the proposed lifting rear window. Porsche had been advised by Reutter that such a feature was 'impossible to completely waterproof'. One feature which was certainly overdue on the road cars from Zuffenhausen was rack-and-pinion steering.

Initial reaction to the car was overwhelmingly favourable. Criticism, however was levelled at a lack of high-speed refinement, certain handling quirks and the price. The first two factors were countered by a process of continual development under the direction of Dr Ernst Fuhrmann; the price factor was solved by the announcement of the 912.

Offered with the new gearbox from the 911, with a choice of four or five speeds, the 912 utilized the 356's four-cylinder 1600cc engine. Detuned slightly in the quest for greater sophistication, the engine gave 90bhp at 4200rpm. The weight saving of 220lbs over the 911, coupled with finer weight distribution, gave exceptionally fine road manners. Due to demand on Porsche's own facilities, the cars were built by Karmann. Production was short, from 1965 to 1968, yet the car was certainly good value in its day.

The fame and fortune of Porsche was built upon the 356 model, which continued in production until the 912 was introduced in 1965, and a great deal depended on the reception accorded to the 911. Engineers Herbert Linge and Peter Falk took a 911 on the Monte Carlo Rally in January 1965, as soon as the six-cylinder model was homologated, and were happy to earn fifth place after a particularly snowy and difficult event.

They could not have guessed that their success would be the first of a string of major victories and world championships for the 911 and its developments.

The 911 itself won the Monte Carlo Rally four times altogether, monopolized such varied events as the Spa 24-Hour Touring Car Race (in 1968 and 1969 two versions of the 911 were homologated as touring, and grand touring, cars!) and the European Grand Touring Championship throughout the 1970s, and dominated the lower places of the World Endurance Championship.

The 911 Carrera RS model became a 'classic' in 1973, the 1000 examples made being sought-after today, and a year later the 911 Turbo model (type 930) was introduced, primarily to homologate the turbocharged engine for competitions.

Three distinct racing models were prepared for the 1976 racing season, and each commanded its field: the 934 faced little opposition in the Grand Touring category, the 935 won the World Championship for Manufacturers after a stern contest with BMW, and the 936 open sports-racing car won the World Sports Car Championship after giving Renault–Alpine a thrashing. The 936 would win at Le Mans in 1976 (Porsche's third victory there), in 1977 and in 1981, but in 1979 the Porsche 935 prepared and entered by Porsche Kremer Racing unexpectedly won the Le Mans race.

The 911's 2-litre, air-cooled, flat six-cylinder engine was enlarged progressively to 2.2 litres (1969), 2.4 litres (1971), 2.7 litres (1973), 3.0 litres (1974), 3.1 litres (1983) and to 3.6 litres in 1988, with power rising from 130 horsepower to 250 horsepower. Such was the progress that while performance increased by leaps and bounds, fuel consumption figures were not impaired.

Turbocharging the 3-litre (later 3.3-litre) engine opened a new range of possibilities, for road customers as well as racing people. From the outset, in 1975, 260 horsepower became an easy, reliable figure for road use, 300bhp coming in 1978 when the 3.3-litre model was introduced, and another 20bhp in 1990.

In 1978, on the race tracks, the same six-cylinder engines were changed to incorporate water cooling for the cylinder heads so that four valves might be fitted into each combustion chamber. Straightaway engine speeds could be raised, and more power could be found with greater thermal efficiency.

When these cylinder heads were applied to the 2.65-litre six-cylinder engine, developed for Indianapolis though not raced there, Porsche had a power unit that would dominate the world's race tracks for nearly a decade. This engine powered the 936 model that Jacky Ickx and Derek Bell drove to victory at Le Mans in 1981, and was the basis of the 956 model (and the subsequent 962) that won the famous 24-hour event every year from 1982 to 1987, taking Porsche's tally to 12.

A variant of the ubiquitous air-cooled engine was certified for aeronautical use (Porsche even developed a variable pitch propellor to go with it), but the sophisticated water-cooled version was installed in the 959 model road cars, each with 450bhp on offer. By 1975 the 911 Turbo was a world-class 'supercar' by any yardstick, and remained so until the 959 came along to set totally new standards. No longer was 160mph impressive as a top speed ... in 1987 you had to boast 190mph or more to impress the neighbours!

Despite having its six-cylinder engine located behind the rear wheels, and despite every square millimetre of the engine compartment being crammed with equipment, the 959 handled astonishingly well, and had brakes that many a racing driver would wish for. At DM420,000 (plus local taxes), it was not cheap, and the cost to Porsche was several times greater. Nonetheless, the 959 was a synthesis of future developments, including the application of a 4-wd system that was announced for the 911 Carrera 4 in 1988.

That six-cylinder engine, admired in 1963 but hardly appreciated, was developed to produce 330 horsepower in normally aspirated form for racing, and more than 800 horsepower in turbocharged form. Always, though, its strongest suit was reliability, testified by 12 Porsche six-cylinder victories at Le Mans, and no fewer than 4 in the Daytona 24-hours in Florida.

Chronology

1964
Deliveries commenced late in the year. 130bhp at 6100rpm from engine type 901.

1966
Carburettors changed from Solex to Weber. After development, the Targa, announced in 1965, was introduced, with a reinforced, folding vinyl panel that could be stowed in the boot. 911 and 912 versions were available. The 911S was announced offering 160bhp at 6600rpm. Front and rear anti-roll bars were standardized. Alloy wheels appeared.

1967
911T introduced offering 110bhp at 5800rpm. The 'T' stands for touring – same interior equipment specifications as the 912. 911L replaced the 911 with trim package similar to the 911S but with power output unchanged. Sportomatic option on all six-cylinder models.

1968
All cars had a 57mm increase in wheelbase, wider wheels and tyres and flared arches. The changes were to aid weight distribution and handling. All models received improved heaters with three-speed fans. Twin batteries in front of the front wheel wells also aided weight distribution. Hydro-pneumatic struts were made optional on the S, which was offered with Bosch fuel injection. Larger ventilated discs on S and E. Self-levelling front struts standard on E and optional on T and S. Power outputs were: 911E, 140bhp at 6500rpm; 911S, 170bhp at 6800rpm.

1969
All models received the 2.2-litre (2195cc) engine. Handling was further improved on the T with optional front and rear anti-roll bars, which also received rear disc brakes, (ventilated on E and S models). Five-speed gearbox standard on E and S models. ZF limited slip differential option. Power outputs were: 911T, 125bhp at 5800rpm; 911E, 155bhp at 6200rpm; 911S, 180bhp at 6500rpm.

1971
All models received the 2.4-litre (2341cc) engine. Power outputs were: 911T, 130bhp at 5600rpm; 911E, 165bhp at 6200rpm; 911S, 190bhp at 6500rpm. 6-inch rims were standardized on the S which also had much detail and trim refinement.

The prototype poses in front of three 356s. Every item was new, from stem to stern, without losing the 'family look'. The glass area was increased by 50%, yet by losing the bulbous look the width was reduced by 10cm.

1972
2.7-litre (2687cc) Carrera RS announced, with weight at 900kg, and output of 210bhp at 6300rpm. 1036 were produced (nominally 1973 cars). Chassis numbers 9113600001 – 9113601036. Sport, touring or racing specs were available to order.

1973
In September the 2.7 engine was standardized. The T and E models were dropped in favour of the 911 and 911S. K-Jetronic injection was adopted for road cars. The top model carried the engine from the 2.7 Carrera RS in a full-weight shell. Power outputs were: 911, 150bhp at 5700rpm; 911S, 175bhp at 5800rpm; 911 Carrera, 210bhp at 6300rpm (the Carrera retained mechanical injection).

1974
930 Turbo introduced at Paris: 2994cc, 260bhp at 3500rpm. Flared arches accommodated 7-inch front and 8-inch rear cast alloy wheels. K Jetronic injection used.

In keeping with company policy, the lines of the 911 resembled those of the 356, although the wheelbase was increased by 100cm and the overall length by 120cm. As can be seen, the prototype featured twin exhausts.

1975
The Carrera 3-litre (2993cc) arrives. K-Jetronic injection allowed 200bhp at 6000rpm. All 1976 models had improved corrosion resistance and one year unlimited mileage warranty.

1977
911 Turbo (type 930) uprated to 2299cc and a full 300 horsepower. The maximum speed rises to 160mph. An air-to-air intercooler is fitted as standard equipment.

The 911SC model becomes the standard 911, replacing the Carrera, with a power output of 180bhp. The engine capacity is 2994cc.

1979
Power of the 3-litre 911 model is increased to 188bhp.

1980
Power of the 3-litre 911 model is increased to 204bhp.

1982
The Cabriolet version of the 911, a full convertible, is announced in Geneva and goes on sale in the summer. The soft-top is well styled and easy to operate.

1983

By increasing the stroke, the capacity of the 911 model increases to 3164cc, and the compression is increased to 10.3:1. The model is named 'Carrera' and the power output is increased to 231bhp.

In September, the futuristic 'Gruppe B' study is shown in Frankfurt, apparently intended for competition use.

1984

René Metge wins the Paris–Dakar 'Raid' in a 911 rally model equipped with a simple 4-wd mechanism, previewing the announcement of the intention to produce the 'Gruppe B' as the 959 model. 200 will be made, for homologation.

1986

René Metge again wins the Paris–Dakar 'Raid', this time in the definitive 959 model with electronically controlled 4-wd, and a twin-turbocharged engine.

The 961, the competitions development of the 959, races to seventh place at Le Mans.

1987

Production of the 959 road car commences, two years late. The car is acclaimed by the motoring pros as the most technically advanced automobile in the world.

The 911 Speedster model is shown in Frankfurt, with production to commence in 1989. The 911 Club Sport arrives meanwhile together with Targa and Cabriolet versions of the Turbo.

1988

The 911 Carrera 4 Coupé model is announced in the summer, with availability early in 1989. The engine capacity is increased to 3.6 litres, the power to 250bhp. Four-wheel drive is a standard feature of the Carrera 4 with its retractable spoiler. 911 Turbo goes 5-speed.

1989

Two-wheel drive version of the 911 Carrera 4 follows. Called the Carrera 2 it is offered with an optional, revolutionary Porsche Tiptronic dual-function gearbox. Targa and Cabriolet versions of the Carrera 4, as well as 2, become available. 911 Turbo production ceases.

1990

Unveiled in Geneva, the new 911 Turbo starts production in the autumn. Only available as a Coupé, it shares the 85% new body design, revised suspension, power assisted steering and ABS braking of the Carrera 2 and 4 but retains the flared wheel arches, fixed rear spoiler and uprated 320bhp engine of its predecessor.

1991

Turbo-look Cabriolet added to the Carrera 2 offering whilst the 260bhp Carrera RS finally enters production after its 1990 Birmingham International Motor Show début.

A quarter of a century later the 911's side profile is virtually identical to that of the 901 prototype in 1963, although the wheelbase was extended by 57mm in 1968.

The 912 engine was essentially similar to that of the 356SC, with modified valve-gear, giving 90bhp at 5800rpm, from a capacity of 1582cc.

The 912 was almost indistinguishable from its 911 stablemate. This is an early model built in 1965, introduced to appease people who still wanted a four-cylinder replacement for their 356s.

The 912 was in production from 1965 until the end of 1968, and is unique in being re-introduced in 1974/5, bridging the gap between the 914 and 924 sports cars.

The 911 model made its competition début in the 1965 Monte Carlo Rally, and driven by Herbert Linge and Peter Falk it finished in fifth place overall.

An early production 911 with negative cambered rear wheels and unflared, slightly hooded, wheel arches.

Björn Waldegaard on the rough in the 1968 Gulf–London Rally. Note the apparently standard appearance of the 911.

Waldegaard again, this time in the Maritime Alps. Following Elford's 1968 Monte Carlo victory, Waldegaard is seen on his way to overall victory in 1969. He won it again in 1970. Ten years after Elford's début win, another 911 took overall honours in 1978.

For the 1968 Daily Express Marathon London to Sydney Rally, Porsche prepared three cars. This example was crewed by Terry Hunter and John Davenport, who failed to finish. The substantial bars were to take the impact should a kangaroo hop into their path!

For some time Vic Elford's name was almost synonymous with rally and racing Porsches. Here he leads Graham Hill at Snetterton on Good Friday, 1967. Damage sustained in an 'off' caused his retirement late in the race.

The Claude Ballot-Lena/Guy Chasseuil 911T passing the well-stocked Porsche factory pit on the way to a second-in-class and eleventh overall result in the Le Mans 24-Hours Race, 1969.

An early 911R, somewhat modified at a later date, with a much later Turbo in the background.

A 911 in its prime. This example won the 1969 *Tour de France* in the hands of Gérard Larrousse and Maurice Gelin. Built in short series expressly for racing, the cars had bodies modified by Karl Baur with glass-fibre boot and bonnet lids. Except for the windscreen, the glass was replaced by Plexiglass. Twin plugs, dry-sump lubrication and twin oil-coolers beneath the headlights helped the 2-litre engine deliver a useful 210bhp at 8000rpm.

Looking remarkably standard, this 2.2-litre car was prepared by Jürgen Barth and his team at Porsche for the 1971 Safari Rally. In all, some 53 modifications were made, including raising the ride height to 26cm and running a 6.5mm thick metal undertray from front to rear.

The 2.4-litre 911ST in which Gérard Larrousse finished second in the 1970 *Tour de France*. The car is a direct descendant of the 911R, with similarly lightened bodywork. Competition weight was a mere 789kg. Larrousse offered the factory mechanics a case of champagne for every kilo they could save below 800kg, and post-event celebrations were joyous!

The 2.4-litre 911S was in production from 1971 to 73. This is the 1972 model, a great favourite, with 190bhp on tap.

Neat and functional, the cockpit layout of the 1972 911.

Early Targas featured a plastic zip-in rear window. Later cars had a glass screen as featured on this 1973 model.

One of the second batch of 500 2.7-litre Carreras. The first run was sufficiently oversubscribed to warrant a further series of 500. The upturned 'ducktail' spoiler is a characteristic of this series, and this example has non-standard bonnet straps fitted, for competitions.

The 3-litre Carrera was homologated for racing on March 1st 1974. In RS form the engine gave 230bhp against the standard Carrera 210bhp. This is the 1974 Geneva Show car. A further development was the RSR, the full race version, with 330bhp.

The Carrera had thinner body panels and retained mechanical injection, while the E and S adopted K Jetronic. The second series featured modified rear suspension mountings.

This machine was built for the 1974 East African Safari Rally, based on a 2.7 Carrera RS. Ride height was increased, all suspension components were strengthened and 'mud ladders' were carried upon the roof. The engine remained standard. Apart from the suspension, most of the Safari model's components remained standard. Björn Waldegaard led almost from start to finish, only to break a driveshaft on the run to the final control and fall back to second place!

Angelo Pallavicini at speed, at Hockenheim in 1975, driving the 1974 Geneva Show car.

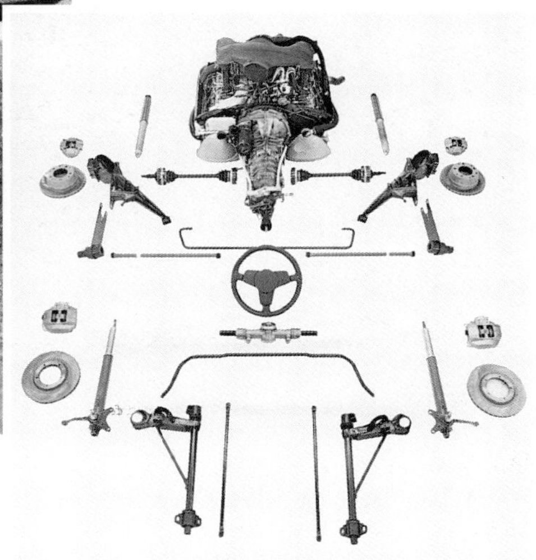

The European Grand Touring Championship was the domain of Porsche customers in the early 1970s. This RS 2.7 is pictured at the Hockenheimring for the 1973 GT Europe meeting, in the livery of Kremer Porsche Racing.

The Carrera RS in action. Here a 2.7 is being driven by Angelo Pallavicini in the 1974 Trento–Bondone Hill Climb.

Introduced at the 1974 Paris Salon, the 930 Turbo (911 Turbo in Great Britain), was partly a homologation exercise and partly a response to the upper market dominance of Italian exotica. The 3-litre engine was fed by KKK Turbocharger and K Jetronic injection, a world first. It was 75kg heavier than the 3-litre Carrera but 10kph faster.

A 930 at speed. The '3' in the type number referred to its turbocharged engine capacity.

The standard 3-litre Carrera had a four or five-speed box dependent on the market. A three-speed Sportomatic was also available. Shown here is a 1980 Targa with five-speed manual.

The engine and luggage compartment of the 3-litre Carrera prepared for racing. Ultimately the normally aspirated engine developed 330bhp, and the model was almost unbeatable in Grand Touring competitions.

Available in coupé and Targa form, the 911SC was the successor to the 3-litre Carrera.

The 3.3-litre Turbo was introduced at the 1977 Frankfurt Show. Recognizable by the larger spoiler, the car offered 300bhp and a top speed of 260kph (162mph). The disc brakes were cross-drilled for better cooling, and were now the same as on the 917 racing cars.

The 3.3-litre 911 Turbo with optional adornment.

With 250bhp at 6800rpm from the 3-litre engine, the 911SC Safari proved an awesome proposition. In the hands of Vic Preston and John Lyall, it took second place in the 1978 Safari.

Ten years after its first Monte Carlo Rally success, Jean-Pierre Nicolas steered his Almeras frères 911 to a fourth victory for the Stuttgart marque in 1978.

The 911SC at the 1982 Geneva Show.

The six-cylinder model was enjoying a new lease of life in the 1980s following a change of management, as Peter W. Schutz gave the 911 total commitment.

In an age of robot production a surprising degree of craftsmanship still goes into the 911. At the time of the picture, in 1982, the factory was producing about 70 cars per day.

A 911 engine ready for installation. Modern emission laws require an amazing amount of 'hardware' to be carried, to clean up the exhaust vapours.

A standard 911SC in 1982 with the star pattern alloy wheels, and 'Martini' stripes recalling the successful racing sponsorship.

A 1982 Targa pictured at the Nürburgring. A popular option at that time was the Fuchs forged alloy wheels with wider, polished rims and Pirelli P7 tyres.

At Geneva in 1982 the first Porsche-built covertible for seventeen years made its début. Deliveries were commenced in the summer and the 911 Cabriolet was immediately sought-after.

After 25 years of production, the 911 remains a highly popular model. This is the Carrera Targa, introduced with the similar coupé at the Frankfurt Show in 1983. Power output was 231bhp at 5900rpm from 3.2-litres. Top speed was quoted as 245kph (152mph). A Spyder version was also announced in 1986.

In 1985 Porsche offered the 'Turbo look' bodywork to 911 customers, and soon the Targa and Cabriolet models were given the wide-body treatment. The Turbo's uprated suspension and braking systems were included in the package.

The Carrera Cabriolet on show for the 1988 Season.

Injecting extra excitement into the range, Porsche introduced the Carrera Club Sport model in 1987, for the 1988 model year. With simplified interior equipment and reduced soundproofing the Carrera CS's weight was reduced by 50kg. The 3.2-litre engine was still rated at 231bhp, but the rev limit was increased to 6840rpm.

Having claimed for years that they couldn't make such a model, Porsche introduced the 911 Turbo Cabriolet for the 1988 model year. The chassis was strengthened to handle the 300bhp on tap.

The Porsche 911 Speedster was a surprising addition to the lineup at Frankfurt in 1987, although production would not begin until 1989. It is, effectively, a Cabriolet with a 356 Speedster style windscreen, and a composite material 'blister' hiding the tonneau.

As soon as the production run of 200 959s had been completed in 1988, Porsche announced the 911 Carrera 4 as an additional model, with permanent four-wheel drive. Its announcement coincided with the 911's 25th anniversary. An increase in capacity to 3.6 litres, and in power to 250bhp, accompany the electronically-controlled 4-wd system derived from the 959.

Jacky Ickx led the Porsche team on the 1984 Paris–Dakar 'Raid', and his car finished sixth after a delay when the wiring overheated.

The first victory by a sports car in the Paris-Dakar Rally took place in 1984, when a Porsche 911, driven by René Metge and Dominique Lemoyne beat the field. As well as contributing to Porsche's prestige, the rally allowed the opportunity of testing a four-wheel drive system for future production purposes.

Long-term Porsche exponent John Fitzpatrick at speed in a Kremer brothers 2.8 RSR at the Nürburgring in April 1973. The English driver won the Porsche Cup in 1972 and 1974 for Kremer, and in 1980 for American entrant Dick Barbour.

Two Carrera RSR 2.8s were entered in the 1973 Le Mans 24-Hour race. Piot/Sbinden in no.44 retired at the 9 hours mark with gearbox problems, while Gregg/Chasseuil in no.48 came home 14th overall.

Peter Gregg and Hurley Haywood won the 1973 Daytona 24-Hour race, a sensational World Championship result for the new 911 RSR. The pairing took the Trans-Am and IMSA titles that year, in the 2.8 RSR.

Gijs van Lennep and Herbert Müller took this Group 5 RSR to victory in the 1973 Targa Florio Race.

Angelo Pallavicini at speed in the 3-litre RSR. On introduction these cars developed 315bhp at 8000rpm, later this was increased to 330 at the same revs. Note the front-mounted oil cooler and the ducts for front brake cooling.

The 934 was the natural successor to the 3-litre RSR. The '3' indicated that the car was turbocharged, the '4' that it was to race in International Group 4. A total of 31 cars were produced. The dry weight was 1120kg, glass windows were required by Group 4 regulations. A 120-litre fuel tank was fitted and the oil tank was moved to the front behind the 908-type oil cooler. Chassis numbers were 9306700151 to 0180 with 0540 completed later in 1976, 9307700951 to 0960 in 1977. The 10 cars built in 1977 gave 540bhp at 7000rpm as opposed to 480bhp of the 1976 cars.

The front compartment of the 934. Note the cross-bracing. As can be seen, the fuel and oil tanks left little extra space.

The 934 engine. The KKK turbocharger was similar to that used on the 917/10. Water was used in the intercooler with two small radiators located behind the front air dam. The second series cars featured a larger turbocharger.

The roll-cage served to create additional torsional stiffness as well as protection for the driver.

The 934 used by Pallavicini to win the Group 4 Championship and take the Porsche Cup in 1978.

Le Mans 1979. The Müller/Pallavicini/Vanoli 934 which came fourth overall and won the Group 4 category.

This 2,142cc Turbo Carrera RSR, campaigned by Gijs van Lennep and Herbert Müller during 1974, was the direct forerunner of the 935. Among its achievements was overall second place in the Le Mans 24-Hour race. Like the 3-litre RSR, the brakes were from the 917. Dry weight was 820kg, power output was put at 500bhp plus.

Jacky Ickx and Jochen Mass drove the factory 935 in 1976 Group 5 events, winning the World Championship for Manufacturers. Usually a second entry was run by the factory; this is Rolf Stommelen at the Nürburgring.

The prototype 935. In later cars the headlights were moulded into a new frontal treatment. The 2857cc engine was based upon the 930 Turbo unit and gave 590bhp at 7900rpm.

Herbert Müller at speed in the twin-turbo version 935 in 1978. In the third season of Group 5 the Porsches faced little opposition, and the factory left the task of winning races largely to the customers.

The Herbert Müller/Claude Haldi 935 on display in 1978. By this time the cars were giving a reliable output of between 600 and 650bhp. Note the clean profile of the engine castings.

Among the private teams running 935s in the late seventies, were the Gelo (Georg Loos) Racing Team. This car was driven by Toine Hezemans/Hans Heyer/Tim Schenken in the 1977 Le Mans 24-Hour race. It retired after one hour with con rod bearing failure.

The Porsche factory wrapped up the 1976 World Championship for Manufacturers with a fine victory at Watkins Glen, achieved by Rolf Stommelen and Manfred Schurti.

...melen/Manfred ... 935/77 at the 1977 Le Mans ...Hour race. The car retired at the four-hour mark with a blown head ...ket.

...second Loos ... until the 22nd hour before retiring ...n seventh place. The Hezemans, Heyer and Schenken driving team ...e co-opted when their own car retired.

The 935 at the 1977 Geneva Show. The rear end treatment is clearly visible, showing the 911 basis beneath the aerodynamic covering.

The fitment of 19-inch diameter wheels and enclosing bodywork made the ugly duckling of 1974 look very purposeful. At the front, the headlamps are fully enclosed as the regulations permitted.

A works shot of the 'Baby'. At its second, and final appearance, at Hockenheim it led from start to finish, driven by Jacky Ickx. It was developed so that Porsche could compete in the 2-litre class, and win once at least, in order to beat the BMWs.

Peter Gregg at high speed, Daytona 1980. On this occasion 'Peter Perfect' was unsuccessful in his favourite race.

The Norisring 1977. The 935/2.0 'Baby' makes its début, weighing in at 750kg due to an alloy spaceframe, and giving 370bhp from 1420cc; the car failed to finish.

Known at the works as 935/78, this car was constructed for the 1978 Le Mans 24-Hour race. Basically, some six centimetres were trimmed from the bottom of the body, giving a smooth lowline appearance. Nicknamed 'Moby Dick', the car finished eighth. The engine was modified to 3.2 litres and featured water-cooled heads. This photo shows the car before entering the paint shop. The doors later reverted to more standard configuration.

At speed in the 1978 24-Hour race, Moby Dick shows its streamlined form. Prior to Le Mans, the 935/78 was driven by Ickx and Mass to an easy victory in the Silverstone 6-hours.

Moby Dick in full war-paint prior to the 1978 Le Mans 24-Hour race.

Driven by Klaus Ludwig and the American Whittington brothers, this Kremer 935K won the 1979 Le Mans 24-Hour race. Although outwardly similar to the factory cars, the Kremer brothers had made several detail modifications and made extensive use of Kevlar.

The Kremer team worked wonders to bring this second 935K into 13th overall. It was driven by Gurdjian/Plankenhorn/Winter.

Another variation on the 935 theme, this time by Claude Haldi. This car finished in eleventh place, slowed by accident damage like many other entries. The race was mostly very wet, and all the important Group 6 entries fell out of the race.

A total of 55 cars took the start at the Le Mans 24-Hour race in 1981. Twenty finished, of which eight were Porsches. This Kremer 935 K3 was driven by Ted Field and Bill Whittington, but they retired with a broken gearbox. The race was won by the 936/81 of Ickx and Bell.

Le Mans 1981. The 935K3 of Dören/Holup/Lassig on blocks in the pits prior to the race. It retired at quarter distance with fuel starvation.

Le Mans 24-Hour race in 1982, John Fitzpatrick and David Hobbs drove to a superb fourth overall in the J David 'Moby Dick'. 956s took the first three places.

The ADAC 1000 Kilometres race in 1981, the Kremer 935K3 of Lundgardh/Plankenhorn/Calvo.

The sensation of the Frankfurt Show in 1983 was Porsche's new 'Gruppe B' sports car, ostensibly aimed at International Group B rallying. The four-valve engine utilized twin turbos to extract 450bhp from 2850cc. Four-wheel drive allows phenomenal acceleration 0-100kph of 3.9 seconds, and a top speed of 197mph. Under the smooth aramid materials bodywork is the familiar 911 shell, but four years would go by before the 959 model would go into limited production; just 200 were made.

The 'Gruppe B' evolved into a Porsche 959 early in 1984 and ideas of turning it into a world-beating rally car were soon dropped when Group B regulations were abandoned. It would win the Paris-Dakar 'Raid' in 1986 as a final stage of development.

Powering the 959 four-wheel drive car is a 24-valve, flat-six engine with water cooled heads, much like the 956/962 racing engine. With progressive twin-turbocharging it develops 450bhp.

The 959 would, rather, become a technological showcase for Porsche's research centre at Weissach, expensive at DM420,000, but very exclusive!

The 1988 model Porsche 911 Carrera Targa retains the classic good looks of the traditional sports car.

The 1988 Carrera Cabriolet, with forged alloy wheels.

The 1988 model 911 Carrera Coupé, with Sport equipment including forged alloy wheels and a matching pair of aerodynamic spoilers.

The 959 driven to victory in the 1986 Paris–Dakar Rally by René Metge and Dominique Lemoyne. For the first and only time in a rally it had the full specification with electronic 4-wd, and the twin-turbocharged engine.

The 1988 911 Turbo: Porsche intended to make 500, but in 14 years the total passed 13,000!

By 1989, the Carrera 4 was in the range and Porsche created this little bit of nonsense to mark Professor Ferry Porsche's 80th birthday, though there was a more serious side to it, too. The Panamericana was a serious development prototype based on the Carrera 4.

Below is the Carrera 4 drivetrain, showing the front differential linked to the rear by a very strong torque tube.

By 1990, the Turbo had taken on a new, less aggressive look, whilst losing nothing of its appeal and performance.

For 1990, the Carrera 4 Cabriolet was the first ever four-wheel-drive open sports car.

The Carrera 2 also joined the model line-up for 1990, seen here in Targa form.

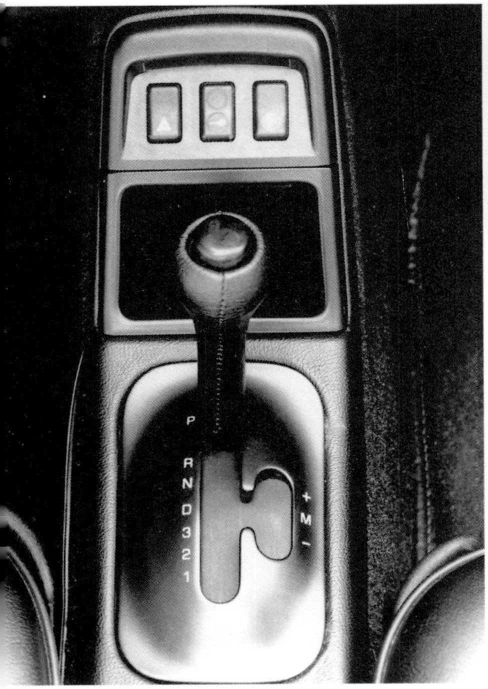

Tiptronic, a vast improvement and logical successor to Sportomatic, was a new form of clutchless transmission, where the driver could simply choose automatic in heavy traffic conditions or select, by "tipping" the gear lever to "plus" for up or "minus" for down-shift. A truly magic transmission, but it still leaves you wondering what to do with your left foot!

THE 914

Given the prevailing condition in the sports car market at the end of the 1960s, a combination of Volkswagen and Porsche expertise in marketing a mid-price, mid-engined car made sound commercial sense. Lotus had used Renault power in its Europa, Fiat had a Ferrari engine powering the Dino while Matra had used Ford power in the 630. From Porsche's point of view, the new car offered their dealers a cheaper product with which to attack lower-priced competition; there was prestige and a positive new product for Volkswagen while the company developed a replacement for the Beetle.

The car made its début at the 1969 Frankfurt Autoshow. A neat mid-engined coupé with a Targa-style removable roof panel, it was announced in two variants, the 914/4 with Volkswagen power, and the 914/6 with the 2-litre version of the 901 engine.

The remarkably clean lines of the car were styled by 'Butzi' Porsche, and it was the Stuttgart company's engineers who designed the 914, using as many production parts as possible. The suspension from the 911 was used at the front, but the rear was a trailing-arm system which owed more to the current Volkswagen. It had little in common with contemporary Super Vee engines beyond configuration. Nonetheless, with 80bhp at 4900rpm and a 0-100kph time of 10.5 seconds, the 914/4 offered reasonable performance.

As for the 914/6, which was half again as expensive, the 1991cc engine delivered 110bhp at 5800rpm, the same output as the original 911T. A five-speed gearbox in both cars offered the prospect of untroubled high-speed cruising, although the company altered the ratios to suit the respective torque characteristics.

In keeping with established practice, the cars were built by Karmann, although the 914/6 was engined and finished at Zuffenhausen. This ensured quality but at a price which left the car at a disadvantage against cheaper and better established mass-producers. Nonetheless, the cars achieved sales success in the all-important U.S. market, although the price of the 914/6 meant that the bulk of sales were of the smaller models.

Given the disappointing sales of the 914/6 it was decided to drop the model in 1972. For those needing extra performance, a Porsche development programme produced a 2-litre fuel-injected version of the 1.7-litre engine. This developed some 100bhp at 5000rpm. Introduced with the new engine were redesigned engine mountings to aid refinement and various other detailed modifications to the sound-proofing. The later models were fine, if somewhat cramped, small sports cars, although the problems of maintaining the mid-engine were never truly surmounted, cutting the potential market for the would-be owner/mechanic. Ferdinand Piëch, head of Porsche's development team, made a final effort to keep the 914/6 alive by building a series of 11 prototype 916 models, with highly tuned 2.4-litre engines developing 190bhp. Predictably, the Porsche shareholders vetoed the project.

On the rally and race tracks, the 914 achieved some success in Group 4 racing and an overall third place on the 1970 Monte Carlo Rally. A small series of competition-modified cars, retrospectively known as 914/6GTs, was laid down. Weight was saved by using fibre-glass for the front and rear covers, plexiglass in the side- and rear-window apertures, and general lightening of the shell and chassis. The arches were flared and the Targa top was reinforced. The 1991cc engine was capable of 220bhp at 8000rpm using 46-IDA Webers and driving through a standard five-speed box.

An early 914. Note the VW hubcaps and wheels. The clean overall shape and neat treatment of the lamps made the four-cylinder model a high volume seller in the States ... but the 'genuine' Porsches were always preferred by six-cylinder customers.

This cutaway illustration of the Porsche 914 shows to good effect the simple layout of engine and transmission. It also illustrates the limits of its design; the angular concept took time to get used to; accommodation was strictly for two.

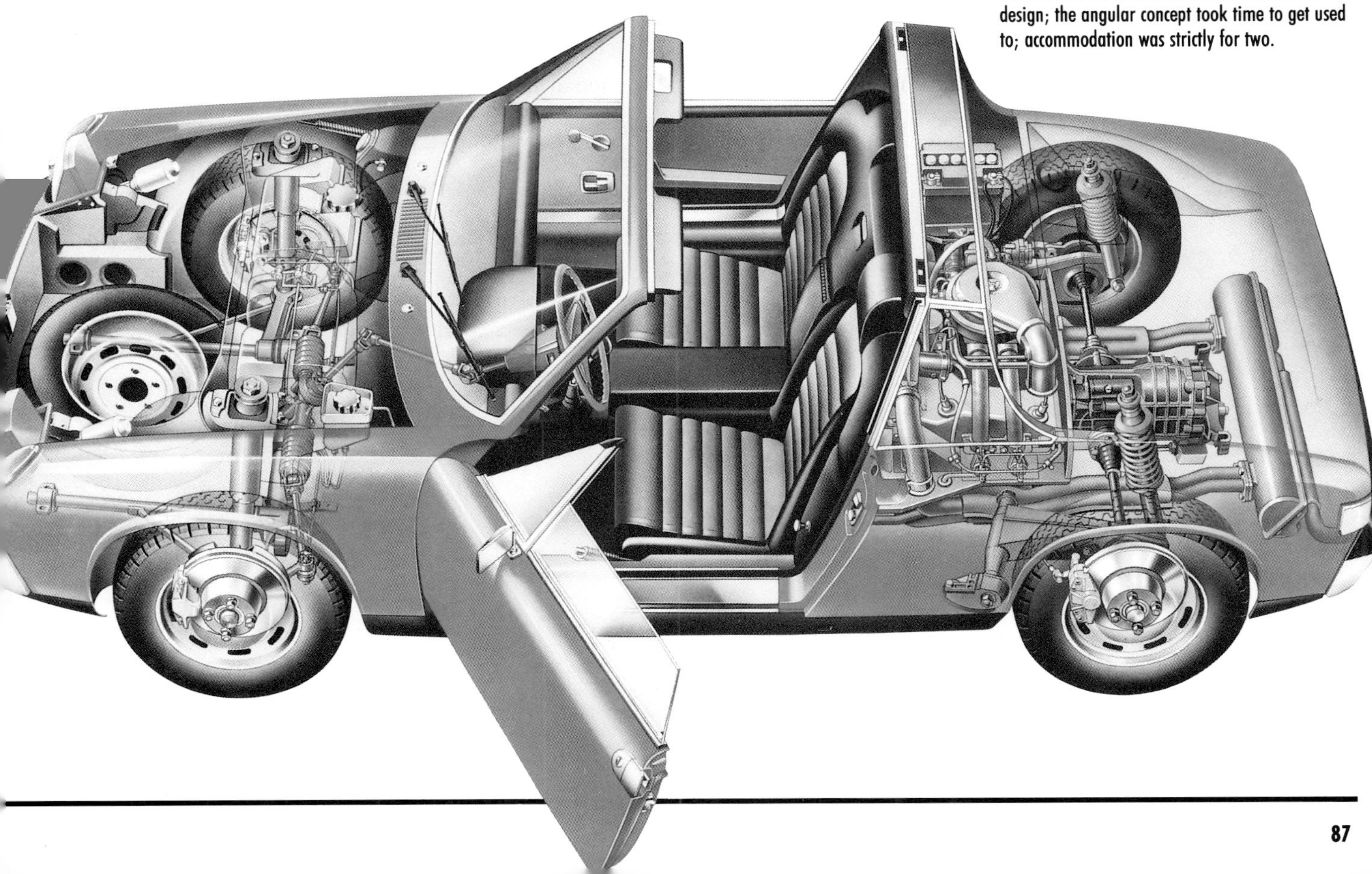

The 914 was built by Karmann. Here, at the 1974 Geneva Show, they have added an eye-catching styling package for the last year of production for the model.

The 914/6 model usually ran on alloy wheels, with 5-stud fixings, the VW powered examples on 4-stud fastened steel wheels.

The superb handling characteristics of the 914 were achieved mainly from fine weight distribution. The narrow-section tyres can be seen on this Swiss registered 914/4.

The 1974 914 2-litre. More comprehensive instrumentation was complemented by neater front and rear bumper styling. Otherwise the car looked remarkably similar to the introductory models. The VW-Porsche 914 series came to an end in 1975 when 115, 646 had been built, and the Porsche 924 was close to introduction.

Eleven 916s were built. The 911S engine was tuned to give 190bhp. Six remained with the works, five were sold to friends of the company. Unfortunately, high production cost killed this potential exotic.

The 1970 914/6 in race trim under the Osnacher banner. Note the Mini-lite wheels used for extra width at the rear. The front track was also increased, as can be seen from the flared arches.

On the occasion of his 60th birthday, Dr. Ferry Porsche was presented with a 914, with a 3-litre, eight-cylinder 908 engine fitted. Only two examples were made, the other, not even de-tuned, version belonged to Dr. Ferdinand Piëch. The car's performance was not unnaturally exciting, with a top speed of 150mph (240kph). The roof was welded into position to improve torsional rigidity.

Snow conditions were ideal for the mid-engined VW-Porsche 914 model with its superb traction and handling.

THE 924

As early as 1970, Volkswagen were assessing the market for a 914 replacement. The project was to build a 2 + 2 using Volkswagen and Audi components which would compete in the area of the market dominated by cars such as the Datsun 240Z and the MGB GT. To this end, a design was commissioned from Porsche to be built at the Audi plant in Neckarsulm. By the time the project reached pre-production stage the management at Volkswagen had changed, Toni Schmücker replacing Heinz Nordhoff. The project was cancelled (although almost ready for production) and Porsche were given the opportunity to buy back the design; they accepted the challenge. Thus was born the 924.

The car was first shown to the public in November 1975. Beneath the smooth shell, designed by Harm Lagaay, was accommodation for four people, although somewhat restricted in the rear, powered by the four-cylinder, water-cooled engine of the contemporary Audi 100. To feed this single overhead cam unit K-Jetronic fuel injection was used, while to keep the front profile low, the engine was canted at an angle of 40 degrees.

When introduced, the car featured a Volkswagen 4-speed gearbox in unit with the rear axle. In 1976 the Audi 3-speed automatic was adapted for the car and, at the same time, the 5-speed version of the manual was offered. Concurrently, a face-lift added a rubber strip along the sides, a voltmeter and an oil-pressure gauge.

The 924 was designed by the young Dutchman Harm Lagaay, supervised by his American boss, Tony Lapine. Shown here is the 1976 model. Although the engine was located at the front, a 51/49 weight balance was achieved by placing the gearbox (transaxle) at the rear.

In early 1977, a special, limited series was produced to celebrate the two world championships won by Porsche in 1976. These cars, like the team cars, were painted in Martini & Rossi colours, with special seats in red with blue surrounds and red carpets. Further refinements included a leather steering wheel and anti-roll bars at the front and rear. The white painted alloy wheels carried 183/700 HR 14 tyres.

For the 1978 model year a 5-speed, Porsche-designed, gearbox was available at extra cost, and the rear suspension and exhaust were redesigned. Other options included electric windows and black painted wheels. On the 24th April, 1978 the 50,000th 924 left the factory.

Announced in November 1978, the 924 Turbo was a much higher performance model with 170bhp, compared with 125bhp for the standard model. Featuring the KKK turbocharger and new cylinder head, these Turbos could be recognized by the air intakes on the bonnet, the 5-stud alloy wheels and the rear spoiler and the leather steering wheel from the 930 Turbo. The seats were in PVC with panels of pseudo-tartan. The instruments had different coloured faces. The cars, which had a 25kph higher top speed, had anti-roll bars front and rear and electric windows as standard equipment.

The four-cylinder Audi 100 engine, with Bosch K-Jetronic fuel injection, was installed at an angle of 40 degrees and produced 125bhp at 5800rpm.

The 1980 models could be recognized by the direction indicators fitted to the front wings' sides. The standard 924 received an anti-roll bar at the front and heavier springs at the rear, while the Turbos had electronic ignition on all cars.

Designed by Porsche designer Anatole (Tony) Lapine, the 924 Carrera GT was introduced at the 1979 Frankfurt Autoshow as a design exercise to gauge public reaction. It continued Porsche's tradition of selling not only racing cars to the public, such as the Carrera 6 and the 917, but also street cars which, like this model, were eligible for rallying and racing in Group 4.

These cars were luxuriously trimmed and were no lighter than the 924 Turbo, but developed 210bhp from 2 litres. Modifications to the engine included an intercooler, a stronger crankshaft and a different cylinder head. The body was modified with polyurethane flared wheel-arches, ventilated discs with 4-piston brake callipers were fitted and the suspension was stiffened up.

For the 1980 Le Mans 24-Hour Race a special 924 was built, the Carrera GT Le Mans. The 2-litre, four-cylinder Audi engine was turbocharged and had an output of 320bhp at 7000rpm. Three cars started in the 24-Hour Race, and all three finished, being sixth, twelfth and thirteenth overall. Following the race a limited series of cars was offered, all painted white with three coloured stripes and the text 'Le Mans'. These cars also had black wheel rims with polished beads, 6J × 15 wheels for 205/60 HR 15 tyres. The rear spoiler of the turbo and a 4-spoke leather steering wheel added to the special treatment.

In 1981, the total production of the 924 was as high as 100 cars per day and on 4th February 1981 the 100,000th car left the factory. For that season, Porsche built two new versions of the 924, the GTS and the GTR; 50 cars of the first type were built, their engines giving an output of 245bhp at 6250rpm. Though the cars offered little comfort, they could still be registered for street use. Not so for the GTR which was built for rally and racing purposes. In rally trim the engine gave 280bhp and in full Group 4 racing trim 375bhp at 6400rpm. The latter version was available from the factory for DM180,000.

The 1982 model used the same steering wheel as the 924 Turbo and Carrera, but a Porsche badge was fitted over the glove-box lock. Besides these modifications the roof load capacity was increased from 35 to 75kg, so that a roof rack with, say, three surfboards could be carried.

The 924 Turbo was cancelled for the 1983 programme following the launch of the 944 model, and the 924 was fitted with the rear spoiler as used on the Turbo, thus reducing the drag from 0.36 to 0.33.

After a life of 10 years in the Porsche 924 (and without any fundamental changes in specification, or power) the Audi-based 2-litre engine was finally abandoned in 1985. The model continued to be produced though, with Porsche's own 2.5-litre counterbalanced four-cylinder engine, slightly detuned and rated at 150bhp so as not to embarrass 944 customers at the lights.

One thing that Porsche could not do was produce the 924S as a 'bargain basement' car, an entry level model that the 924 was in the 1970s, and inevitably demand dwindled. Customers preferred to spend a little more and buy a 'real' 944. The 924S was discontinued in the summer of 1988, and from then on the Stuttgart firm would concentrate on expensive and up-market models, with the total annual production reduced from circa 50,000 to, perhaps, 30,000 cars.

Rear three-quarter view of the 1976 model. The large, moulded rear screen needed a wiper which was late in coming; later models also offered a small spoiler which improved high-speed stability.

The only external modification evident on the 1977 models was a hard rubber strip along the side of the body.

Jürgen Barth, Porsche racing driver and employee, drove this 924 rally car in the 1979 Monte Carlo Rally. The bodyshell was actually a Turbo, but carried the normal engine. (The Turbo had yet to be homologated.) The car finished twentieth overall, fourth in its class.

Though the body of the Turbo is similar to that of its normally aspirated brother, the car can be recognized by the four air intakes between the headlights and the NACA duct in the bonnet. Note the 5-stud alloy wheels, rear spoiler and rear screen-wiper.

Special 924s were built for the American SCCA races to compete with the Datsun 240Z and Triumph TR7. The stripped cars had a weight of 970kg and their 2-litre engines developed 180bhp at 7000rpm.

The two-tone colour scheme effectively lowered the waistline of the Turbo, giving it an opulent and racy air complemented by Porsche alloy wheels. Interiors, too, were fairly spectacular, lifting what was to have been a cut-price exercise into the luxury bracket.

With 170bhp available from the turbocharged 2-litre engine, Porsche's 924 Turbo became a sought-after model, but lacked volume because it was not exported to America.

The 924 Turbo as seen at the 1979 Geneva Motor Show.

The bare essentials of the 924 Turbo. The torque tube formed an integral part of the structure of the car.

Seen at the 1978 Geneva Motor Show: the internals of the 924 Turbo. The 170bhp four-cylinder engine made the 924 the most powerful sports car in its class.

The 924 Turbo seen at the 1982 Geneva Show in the new Expo centre near the airport. The engine was uprated to 177bhp in 1981 and the car was given further refinement – the model is recognized by the flap over the filler cap.

The 924 Turbo was equipped with Porsche's own 5-speed gearbox between the rear wheels, rather than an Audi-VW manual or automatic transmission.

In the 1979 East African Safari this 924 Turbo was driven by Jürgen Barth. The engine had a standard output of 170bhp at 5500rpm, but the entry retired with running gear problems. Later on Barth competed in the Rheinhessen Rally in Germany with a 924 Turbo, finishing in 14th place.

DATACOM DB/DC
HEIGO
LB-ZL 366

Whenever Porsche uses the name Carrera, it means that the specific car can be used both in the street and for professional racing (see the earlier 356 Carreras, the 911s and so on). A prototype of the 924 Carrera was shown at the Frankfurt Autoshow in 1979. The car was highly equipped, and had wider wings to allow wider tyres. The front arch extensions and spoilers were made of deformable RIM plastic. The 924 Carrera GT had a top speed of 240kph (149mph). The car could easily be recognized by the air intake on the bonnet and the wide wheel-arches.

DETA
Castrol

At the end of 1979, Porsche started to build some special 924GTR cars for the 1980 Le Mans 24-Hour race. Three cars started and all three finished. This is the car driven by the British drivers Andy Rouse and Tony Dron. They finished twelfth overall.

1981 marked thirty years of Porsche participation at Le Mans. That year the race was won by a 936/81 driven by Ickx and Bell. This 924GTR Carrera was driven to eleventh overall by Manfred Schurti and Andy Rouse.

For the 1000 Kilometre race at the Nürburgring in 1981, Canon Racing entered this 924GTR which was driven by Richard Lloyd and Tony Dron.

entscheidet
Z-H 8522
43
Canon
GORDON RAMSAY PORSCHE
Can

The 924GTS was introduced for the 1981 racing season. Fifty were built and prepared for Group 4 competition. It had a top speed of 250kph (155mph) and accelerated to 100kph in 6.2 seconds. It is shown here with a 924 behind it, prior to a demonstration run at the Nürburgring. The factory extracted some 375bhp from a turbocharged, four-cylinder Audi engine as fitted in the 924GTR.

In 1981 Walter Rohrl, the World Rally Champion, and Christian Geistdorfer drove a 924GTR in selected European rallies. The car was prepared by the Porsche factory, but was operated by Schmidt Motorsport.

After a 10-year run the 2-litre 924 was phased out in 1985, and replaced by the 924S model powered by Porsche's own 2.5-litre four-cylinder engine. The 924 model was finally discontinued in 1988.

A factory publicity photo showing the 1982 model 924 next to the 924 Turbo, clearly showing the differences.

Celebrating Porsche's 12th victory at Le Mans, a special version of the 924S model was produced (just as a special 924 was made after Porsche's fourth success in 1977!). This proved to be the final production year for the 924 model.

PORSCHES IN COLOUR

In these next few pages are Porsches in colour - road cars, race cars, rally cars. Here are some of the most exciting cars in the world, regardless of maker, alongside some of the more ordinary Porsches (as ordinary as a Porsche can be, that is).

These photographs serve to confirm the excitement of Porsche - in all its forms.

Porsche number 1. The mid-engined aluminium-bodied prototype built in Gmünd, seen here at the 1981 anniversary meeting. The car still retains a temporary chassis repair, the result of a testing accident in 1947.

A factory shot of a 1962 Carrera II, one of the enduringly desirable 'hotter' versions of the 356. Note the very period pastel colour.

A 356A, looking exceptionally standard compared with today's heavily modified rally machines, prepares for the 1959 Monte Carlo Rally.

A genuine 1966 911R photographed in 1981. The owner has sensibly resisted the temptation to 'update' the car, thus it clearly demonstrates mid-sixties racing practice with its fairly narrow wheels and original spotlamps.

Twenty-one years into its production career the 911 shape was still showing no signs of ageing. This 1984 911SC is seen at the Hockenheimring.

The 1975 Carrera 3 litre was a direct road going descendant of the 1973 3.0 RSR. Georg Loos campaigned this particular RSR in the GT class yet managed several overall high placings.

A logical step from the 3.0 RSR was the 934. This example, owned by Richard Cleare, one of endurance racing's last gentleman entrants, carried him and ex-works driver Tony Dron to class honours in the 1982 Le Mans 24 hours.

America became the happy hunting ground of the 914. This works shot clearly demonstrates the squared off early-seventies lines which, unlike the 911's, have tended to date.

The Audi that never was. On introduction the 924 suffered at the pens of the motoring press, who seemed to expect a far more refined car. It survived to become the largest selling model ever to bear the Porsche crest.

Le Mans has always been the proving ground of Porsche. Following a sensational 1981 debut with the 924 GTP, the factory entered two of these 924 GTRs for 1982. Unfortunately success eluded them that year, so marking the last Sarthe appearance of these 'junior' works cars.

Geneva 1978 saw the 928 gleaming sexily on the Porsche stand. Initial reaction was mixed, although a heavy German presence was enough to vote the 928 'Car Of The Year'.

In outward appearance the 944 certainly owed much to the 924 GTP. It fitted into the range neatly between the 924 and the cheapest 911, offering a full house Porsche 2.5 litre engine for the purist who wanted something more than the Audi 2 litre unit of the 924. The press received the car ecstatically.

Turin 1984. The startling 959 appears as 'a design exercise'. It was a direct response to the four wheel drive supercar trend which began with the Audi Quattro and spawned a whole new breed of production based rally and race cars.

Almost simultaneously with the announcement of a limited homologation run of 959s this machine arrived and, with a similar sister, pulverised the opposition on the 1986 Paris–Dakar.

Edgar Barth, seen here in the RSK 718/8 he took to class honours in the European Championships with Herbert Linge. The venue is Le Mans 1963. Chassis no.-718.047.

Hillclimbs have always held a higher profile in European motorsport than they have in the UK. Porsche dominated the European championship from the mid-1950s to the mid-1960s with the 550 Spyders and then their direct descendants the RS60 and 61. This particular RS61, with an early flat 8 2 litre 771 engine, was nicknamed Grandmother. With it Edgar Barth won the European Hillclimb Championship in 1963 and 1964.

Le Mans 1963 and these two Arbarth Carrera 2000GS were entered in the smaller category. The nearest car is chassis number 122.992, handled for that race by Schiller and Pon. The distinctive Kamm tailed bodywork earned the cars the nickname 'wedges'.

Le Mans 1965. The 275 LM (6119) of Spoerry sits behind the little 904 GTS 4 of Rolf Stommelen. The visual impact of the little 2 litre cars almost keeping pace with larger engined machinery was massive.

Le Mans 1967. Poirot drives one of five factory 906s . The previous year these cars had taken the Index of Performance, four of five works entries finishing in the top seven places.

This 907/6 took 5th overall first time out at Le Mans in 1967, driven by Hans Herrman and Jo Siffert.

The 910/6 was almost an accident of design. It used technology from the concurrent Lotus F1 cars as well as the 906. Never intended for general homologation, a rule change in 1968 allowed owners to use them in sportscar racing classes. This example failed to run the distance at the 1967 Le Mans but later took victory in the Targa Florio running in the prototype class.

One of the all time greats. A 908/2 seen on an Italian test track. The cars stayed competitive right through until the 1980s aided by some appallingly inept international rule changes.

The arrival of the 917 finally elevated Porsche into the stuff of motor racing legends. The full homologation run was lined up outside the factory for the inspection of FIA inspector Dean Delamont.

The smart blue and orange livery of the Gulf Porsche. John Wyer, the JW of JW Racing, had made the livery famous on Ford GT40 and Mirage cars prior to the agreement with Porsche.

Gulf
Gulf
1

The PA (Porsche–Audi) Spyder which Jo Siffert campaigned in Can-Am 1969–70.

The 917 KH of 1970. Note the difference in bodystyle wrought after the ad-hoc 'research' of David Yorke and the JW team mechanics.

Porsche Salzburg, run by Ferdinand Porsche's daughter, Louise Piech, was the main rival of the Gulf JW team. In 1971 they became the Martini Porsche Team. Here the aerodynamic development of the Lh cars can clearly be seen.

With the demise of Can-Am the only type of racing left open to the 917 was Inter-Series. Here a 917-10 is seen at speed.

Following the tragic death of Jo Siffert at Brands Hatch, Mark Donohue took up the Can-Am challenge. Here he is running at speed in the 917-30 which in his hands, and those of George Follmer, caused a change in Can-Am rules.

A fairly academic rule change led to the replacement of the 956 by the slightly modified 926. Here Derek Bell and Jacky Ickx head for Le Mans laurels in 1985

For the eighties the 956 arrived to carry the Porsche racing challenge. Unfortunately there was little opposition, a fact which allowed the various private entrants to get onto even terms with the works. One of the more successful was the British team run by Richard Lloyd and using the services of F1 pilot Dr Jonathan Palmer. Here the car is being refuelled at Le Mans 1985.

The first 911 Turbo was introduced in 1974, and soon set the standards by which others were judged. This 1988 model, although outclassed following the arrival of the 959, still carried the flag by virtue of being available and 'relatively affordable'.

1974 2.7 Carrera RS Touring – a driver's delight and a collector's dream.

Carrera RS and a 1988 Carrera Club Sport belie their sixteen-year age differential.

In 1975 the Austrian government belatedly recognised the cultural contribution which Ferdinand Porsche had made by issuing this stamp commemorating the 100th anniversary of his birth.

By 1989, Teo Fabi was driving this March-Porsche single-seater in the Indy Car Series in the United States, though not with great success. Whilst Fabi won the 1989 Mid-Ohio Race, 1990 did not prove a vintage year.

A studio shot of the Footwork Arrows FA12, which sadly did not make the grade for Porsche, who withdrew from Formula 1 before the heady days of the TAG-Porsche powered McLarens were eclipsed.

Here's the Footwork car pictured during tests at Silverstone in November 1989.

By the end of 1991, having suffered a savaging in the economic downturn, Porsche sprang back with a line-up of magnificent cars for the next year, heralded here by the 3.6 Carrera RS.

Also in the 1992 line-up came the Carrera 2 Cabriolet in Turbo-Look......

......then 1992 had another treat in store for Porsche fans, in the form of the superb new 968. Heir to the mantle of the 924 and 944 series cars, this new coupé was a worthy successor to the role of "entry-level" Porsche.

There was a 968 Cabriolet, too, which looked slightly chunky from behind, but still pleasing, except perhaps to the person whose "car in front" is quickly becoming "the car behind".

Forgetting the air bag system on this left-hand drive model, the 968's interior is identical to the 944 Series it replaces apart from minor detail alterations which include an analog clock in the compartment below the stereo radio/cassette player and an outside temperature read-out where the digital clock used to be. The stitched-seam design of the interior door panels, which forms a continuation of the dashboard, is another feature shared with the 911.

Under the bonnet, there doesn't seem much room for anything else but the engine, though Porsche have managed to squeeze in a turbo for 1993.

THE 944

When Audi produced its five-cylinder, 2-litre engine, the obvious inference was that sooner or later the four-cylinder unit which powered the 924 would be phased out. Faced with this prospect the design team responded by developing their own replacement. This unit was in essence a single bank of cylinders from the 928 V8, as first seen in a modified 924GTP at Le Mans in 1981. The unit was turbocharged and featured Bosch-programmed injection. For racing purposes it used twin camshafts to activate four valves per cylinder. To offset the inherent vibration from an oversquare 2.5-litre four-cylinder engine it used toothed rubber belts to drive counter rotating shafts mounted on the side of the block.

These shafts, a variation of the Lanchester harmonic balancing principle, were carried over into the road car. Perhaps understandably, the twin cams and turbochargers were not. The standard 944 featured a single overhead cam and the more normal two valves per cylinder. The engine was the first to adopt Porsche's own TOP cylinder head design, this being used in conjunction with Bosch L-Jetronic digital electronic injection to allow a massive torque yield from a compression ratio of 10.6:1.

In appearance, although the car obviously used the bodyshell of the 924, larger flared wings, a front air-dam and all-uprated interior specification enhanced the appeal, along with eye-catching new-style alloy wheels carrying 205/VR 55 tyres on 7J × 15 rims. Porsche forged-alloy 16-inch wheels were an option. On introduction the car was capable of 0-100kph in 8.4 seconds and a top speed of 220kph (137mph).

In its first full year of production, to August 1983, the 944 smashed all previous records for a single model, as 23,200 were produced, each one with an engine manufactured and tested in Zuffenhausen, an all-important feature for Porsche's clientèle.

The début of the 16-valve, turbocharged prototype at Le Mans in 1981 was obviously a glimpse into the future, the development of a turbocharged version, albeit an 8-valve version, being unveiled in due course. The 944 Turbo with 220bhp

This 924 GTP with a race-modified 944 engine was entered by System Porsche for the 1981 Le Mans 24-hours. Driven by Jürgen Barth and Walter Röhrl, it ran reliably to seventh overall and third in its class. The entry was also awarded a prize for the least time spent in the pits, 56 minutes being the least possible for 21 refuelling stops at a controlled rate.

The cylinder head of the Le Mans car showing the belt-driven twin cams and other details. In the left-hand picture the drilled and ventilated racing disc-brakes can be seen to good effect. Although the engine was designated 944, the car was entered as a Porsche 924 GTP since the announcement of the 944 model was still a couple of weeks away! Porsche's management has ruled out a 16-valve turbocharged 944 model, on the grounds that the engine bay would have to be changed substantially.

was announced in February 1985, and the 16-valve 944S with 190bhp came in the summer of 1986, effectively being one half of the 928S4's V8 motor.

Substantial changes, including ABS as standard, were announced for the 944 series in the summer of 1988 (1989 model year) following the discontinuation of the 924S model. The 'standard' 944 model had its engine increased in capacity to 2681cc as a result of increasing the bore dimension to 104mm. Power rose only slightly, to 165bhp. but the torque figure was improved usefully.

The 16-valve 944S2 model had the larger 104mm bore but its stroke was increased to 88mm. The capacity rose to 2990cc and the power to 211bhp, endowing the car with a genuine 150mph top speed. The 944 Turbo's chassis was adopted with ventilated discs front and rear, uprated suspension and more effective underbody aerodynamic aids.

Finally, the 944 Turbo Cup racing model's 250bhp engine became standardized in the 944 Turbo itself, the engine capacity remaining at 2479cc. Its top speed now matched the 911 Turbo's, at 161mph.

Production of the Coupé version of the 944S2 in 1989 was soon joined by the Cabriolet variant. Such was the success of these two new models that the 944 ceased production that summer followed a year later by the 944 Turbo. The latter was regarded by many as the best all-round Porsche but never realised its full sales potential.

The 1981 Porsche 944, photographed at the Nürburgring, quickly became the fastest-selling car in Porsche's history. With the counterbalanced engine designed at Weissach, it was, at last, a 'proper Porsche'.

The aluminium 2.5-litre, four-cylinder 944 engine. Early reactions were that the counterbalanced unit was as smooth as a six-cylinder, perhaps a rival for an 'eight'.

A snow-white 1981 944 demonstrator, embellished by a Swiss dealer, who would probably like to forget his handiwork now!

It took 42 Porsche apprentices 2000 hours to build this cutaway 944, shown at the 1982 Geneva Motor Show.

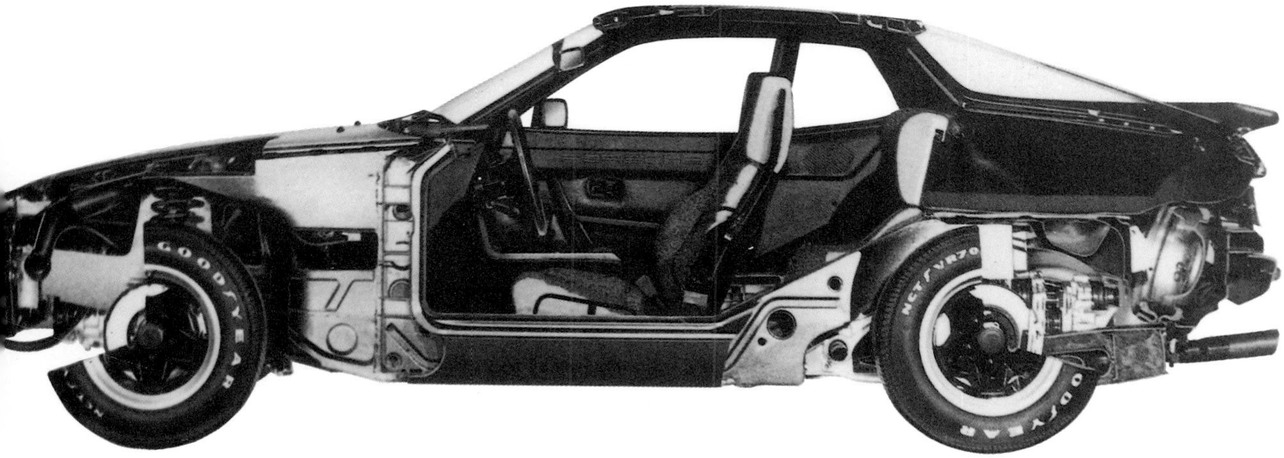
GOODYEAR

Porsche 944 for the 1983 model year, with forged alloy wheels.

The Porsche 944 in 1986 trim with 928-style wheels as standard equipment.

The 944 Turbo was officially introduced at the 1985 Frankfurt Motor Show. It was, at that time, the first in the world to develop the same power (220bhp) with or without catalytic equipment.

The Turbo model's polyurethane nose panel was much more aerodynamic than the 944's, and the rear undertray was new.

S HV 4549

turbo

The exhaust system on the 944 Turbo engine passes to the back of, and below, the flywheel in order to position the KKK turbocharger close to the inlet manifold. The turbo has a water jacket to ensure that it runs cooler and has a longer life.

The 1985 version of the 944 was improved in many details: a new windshield was bonded to the body, new 7-inch wheels were fitted and the tuel tank was enlarged from 66 to 80 litres. A completely new dashboard with an elliptical shape got rid of the last remnant of VW's heritage.

The sleek 944 Convertible was first seen at Frankfurt in September 1985 in prototype form which survived extremely well through the transitional stages leading to production. Deliveries did not commence until January 1989 as the American Sunroof Corporation had to build a new factory to produce the tops.

In 1985, the 944 Turbo finally arrived, followed in 1986 by this, the 944S. Using four valves per cylinder the car offered even smoother power delivery than the original 944. It offered 190bhp with, or without catalytic equipment and superb top-end performance, though it had little advantage over the 8-valve model below 4000rpm.

In 1987 the recently announced 944S 16-valve coupé was equipped with the rear undertray of the Turbo model, improving aerodynamic efficiency.

The 944S2s in Coupé and Cabriolet guise became the 944 Series mainstay from the 1991 model year. The folding tops were made and fitted by the American Sunroof Corporation, at a new factory near Stuttgart.

In 1973 Porsche made a statement about philosophy, expressed by the Long Life car at the Frankfurt Show. It was not a prototype in any sense, but a synthesis of ideas for making a car with an almost indefinite life span. Within two years Porsche's sports models were made largely of galvanized steel, and in 1977 the 928 model was made almost entirely of galvanized steel, alloys, plastics, rubber and other non-corrodible materials.

THE 968

The end of the long-term contract with Audi to build the Porsche four-cylinder range of sports cars at Neckarsulm proved an opportune time for Porsche to introduce a new model.

Furthermore, with production down to 32,362 units in the preceding financial year and falling, it also made commercial sense for the company to integrate all assembly in-house at Stuttgart-Zuffenhausen. Henceforth, all Porsches could be called pure Porsches.

Right-hand drive production of 944S2s ceased in December 1990 and the last left-hand drive 944S2s left Neckarsulm in early March the following year. A few more were destined to be assembled at the ancestril home prior to the arrival of its successor.

Planned some two and a half years previously, the new Porsche 968 was very much perceived as an evolutionary model. Its 944 heritage was plain to see but it embodied a determined effort to stamp a pure Porsche identity in terms of design, engine and transmission technology and environmental compatibility.

Body styling was again the work of Harm Lagaay and his team. The original 924 body designer was now head of the design studio and his feeling that Porsche required a strong model identity across the complete range was clearly evident.

The 911 was and always would be everyone's conception of a true Porsche sports car. Thus, the new 968 received a new front-end treatment. Gone was the somewhat angular design of the 944 series to be replaced by large round headlamps, a sloping bonnet and curved wings. The rear of the car also differed from its predecessor with its smooth design treatment embracing uniform rear light clusters. In between the integral front and rear tail sections, made of deformable polyurethane and concealing the bumpers, the sides featured low-slung polyurethane sill extensions and integrated stone guards first seen on the Carrera 4. Colour-coordinated 'Turbo' mirrors and door handles completed the function-orientated Porsche design philosophy.

At the heart of the new 968 was the familiar 3-litre, in-line, water-cooled, four-cylinder light alloy engine with its twin counter rotating balance shafts. However, the 16-valve unit had been uprated to 240bhp and boasted a massive torque yield of 305Nm at 4100rpm. The combination of a new intake manifold with bypass passage and the unique patented Porsche VarioCam camshaft timing system were primarily responsible for providing the 3-litre engine with more torque than any similar capacity normally aspirated engine in the world, the latter accounting for 40Nm.

Power transfer was again by connecting tube to either a rear-mounted new standard six-speed manual gearbox or optional four-speed Porsche Tiptronic dual-function transmission system. Both set new standards in terms of sporting or economical driving style.

Independent suspension, identical in layout to the earlier 944 series, was provided by light alloy wishbones and McPherson struts, coil springs, twin-tube gas-pressure dampers and an anti-roll bar at the front and light alloy semi-trailing arms, transverse torsion bars, double acting hydraulic dampers and an anti-roll bar at the rear. The damping itself was closer to the previous 944 Turbo than the 944S2 to provide a firmer but more tractive ride. New generation eye-catching open style 7J and 8J x 16 light alloy rims carried respectively 205/55 ZR 16 and 225/50 ZR 16 tyres.

A race proven ABS braking system including 4-piston, fixed caliper ventilated disc

The shape of the four-cylinder Porsche of the nineties - more rounded flowing lines leave the 944 series behind.

brakes front and rear could be relied upon to stop the new 968 from 0 - 100kph in less than three seconds.

The optional Sport suspension package allowed for even larger front brakes to be fitted as well as providing chassis height and and shock absorber adjustment, stiffer springs, larger diameter anti-roll bars and 7.5J and 9J x 17 rims carrying 225/45 ZR 17 and 255/40 ZR 17 tyres. The larger 17" rims had an asymmetric lip on the outside which prevented tyre slippage due to sudden drop in air pressure, even when cornering.

With an identical wheelbase plus front and rear track to the earlier 944 series, the

The integral front nose section of the new 968 is typically Porsche with its two horizontal air intakes and single radiator apertures plus carefully blended-in auxiliary lamps. The bumper is concealed behind the deformable polyurethane panel.

chassis specification allied to the Transaxle layout, for optimum weight distribution front to rear, ensured the new 968 furthered Porsche's reputation for providing the driver with a fine handling sports car.

Acceleration to 100kph was achieved in 6.5 seconds using the manual six-speed version whilst the optional Tiptronic took a further 1.4 seconds. Top speeds were respectively 156 and 153mph.

Remarkably, despite being heavier and producing more power and torque, the 968 was actually more fuel efficient than the 944S2 it succeeded. A key factor was the use of a 'hot wire' measurement of air mass working in conjunction with the Bosch Motronic engine management system.

New for Porsche was the reflector system on the round pop-up headlamps which provided variable focus for greatly increased light output. The integrated auxiliary driving and fog lamps also benefited from special reflectors, the latter improving illumination of the road sides by 30% and preventing dazzle in fog. At the rear, adoption of uniform red light clusters was made possible through use of special optics and filters which produced the regulation variable light colours.

Attention to detail on the 968 was exemplified by the neat little compartment at the front of the engine bay which housed a pair of white service gloves. Regrettably this did not extend to the interior which remained unchanged from the earlier 944 generation apart from a few token gestures which included 911 style interior door panels and armrests.

The new Porsche 968 was announced in the summer of 1991 and shown for the first time at that year's Frankfurt Autoshow. Production commenced later that year

Overall, the new 968 Cabriolet is less like the 944 Series than the new Coupé. Note that the absence of side mouldings and adoption of new aerodynamically shaped door mirrors, colour co-ordinated door handles and polyurethane sill extensions all help to differentiate an otherwise standard 944 Series side profile.

At the heart of the new 968 is an uprated three-litre, 16-valve, 240bhp, water-cooled, in-line, four-cylinder engine with unique VarioCam camshaft timing. At 305Nm, the engine currently boasts more torque than any other three-litre, normally-aspirated production car engine.

and coupé and cabriolet versions rolled off the Stuttgart-Zuffenhausen assembly lines in the same wide choice of colours and interior trims as was previously only obtainable with the 911 and 928 series.

The same combination of modern automated technology and traditional handcraft skills were employed with the exception that the 'white' bodies were produced by Karmann whilst the American Sunroof Corporation continued to be retained to produce the cabriolet tops.

As most world markets rode on the bottom of an economic recession the success of the 968 would prove of critical importance to Porsche's future against ever-increasing competition.

THE 928

In 1972, the factory began planning a replacement for the 911. Under Dr Ernst Furhmann the decision was made to make the car a front-engined, water-cooled vehicle, embodying the very latest technology. A prime requisite was that the car should be capable of development in the same manner as the 911. This was vital in view of increasing world-wide legislation on pollution and crash resistance. The result was the 928.

Introduced at the Geneva Show in 1977, the car aroused considerable attention and admiration, and was the recipient of the 1978 Car of the Year award. A true Porsche, with a V8 engine of 4474cc, a rear-mounted, 5-speed gearbox and a body shell incorporating the last word in deformable structure technology, the car seemed a radical departure from the traditional image.

Beneath the ultra-smooth skin, however, Porsche had stayed close to tried and tested suppliers. The engine, which was of light alloy construction, incorporated a crankshaft from Alfing, pistons from Mahle and Schmit and the sintered steel conrods came from GKN. The two overhead cams were driven by a Pirelli toothed rubber belt and the tyres were P7s. The engine was fed by the K-Jetronic injection from Bosch, who were later to add the ABS braking system. In every respect the material and build quality of the 928 was beyond reproach. Even the deformable front and rear RIM plastic sections were coloured with a newly-developed elastic paint to resist impact cracks.

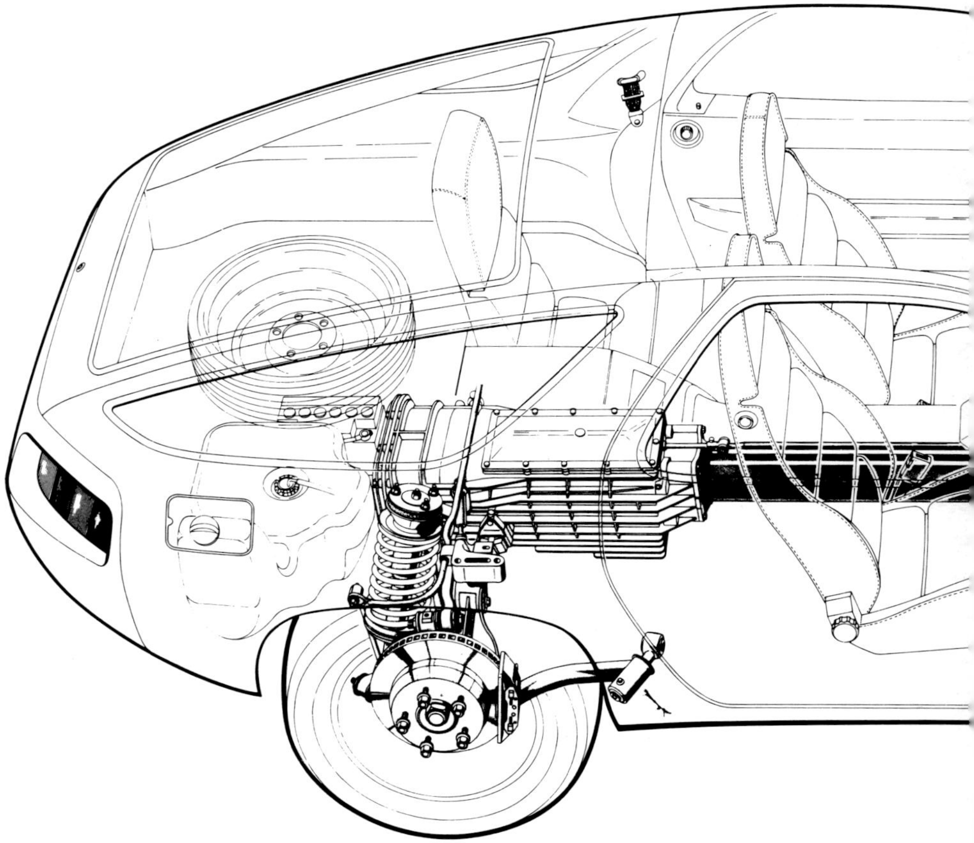

Cutaway of the original 928 showing how the main components have been spaced for even weight distribution. The Porsche 'Weissach' rear axle with 'toe' correction probably led the way to most Japanese manufacturers adopting four-wheel steering on high performance models.

Once the body has been fully trimmed, protected and the electrics installed, it is mated to the pre-assembled running gear. Although the car incorporates an ever-increasing degree of technological sophistication, the fine craftsmanship of the Swabian workforce is still evident in the beautiful detailing and the fine finishing.

The cars remained unchanged for 1977 and 1978. For 1979 the 928S arrived offering 300bhp at 5900rpm against the standard car's 240bhp at 5500rpm in European trim. Both the 928 and the 928S benefited from a raise in compression ratio from 8.5:1 in the early standard cars, to 10:1 in the post-1979 models. As well as this, the capacity of the S was increased to 4664 by an increase of 2mm in the bore, and the ventilated disc brakes were uprated.

Planning for the 928 started in 1972, and during the five years to its introduction in 1977, many cars were equipped with 928 parts for testing. One such was this Audi Coupé which carried the engine and transmission for over 100,000 kilometres. Due to the excess width of the 928, the Audi was sliced lengthways and widened by 11cm.

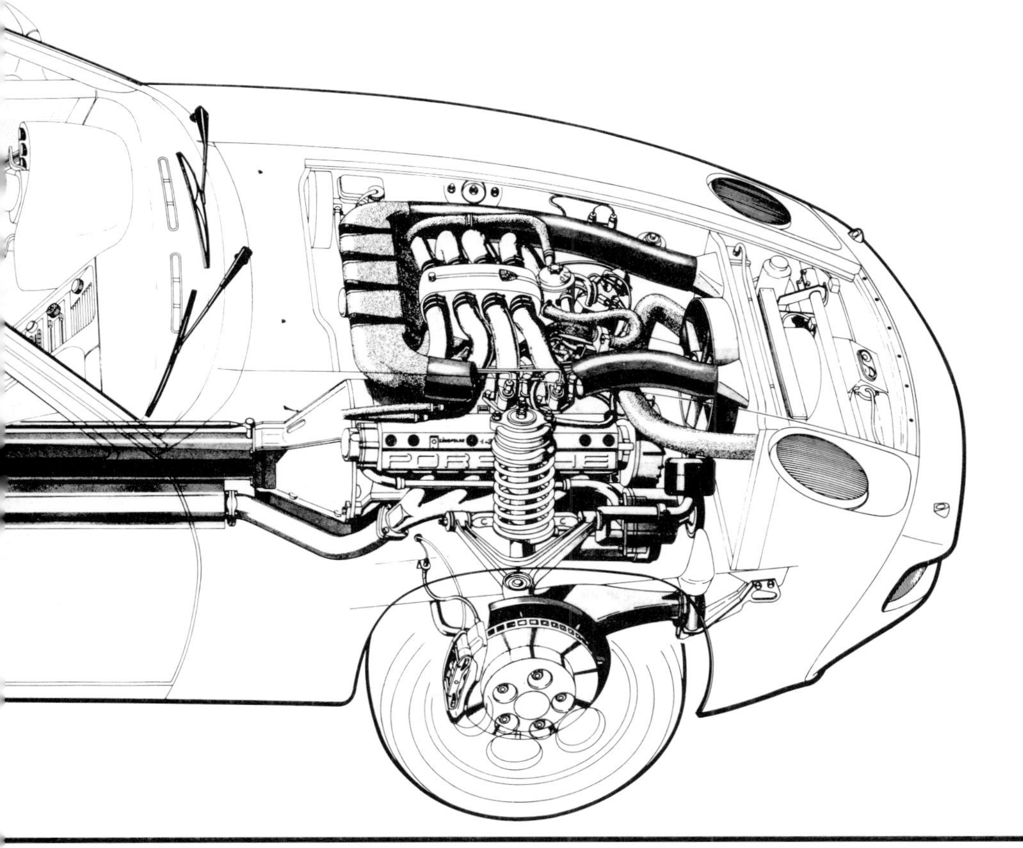

Elsewhere, the 928S remained similar to the standard car. The transverse unequal wishbones at the front and rear, coupled with forward reaching links with in-built compensation at the rear, were totally adequate to cope with the extra power, as was the rear-mounted gearbox. The rubber wear, 225/50 VR 16, was also adequate, although as the car was specifically designed around the tyre characteristics, that was hardly surprising.

Substantial changes were carried out on the 928S model in 1983, when the original 4.5-litre version was discontinued. The new Bosch LH Jetronic 'hot wire' injection system was adopted, metering the fuel/air mixture more precisely, and the power rose to 310bhp. The torque figure rose too, and the car's maximum speed became 158mph (253kph).

The automatic version showed a further gain in performance with the adoption of Daimler–Benz's new four-speed transmission, with a more suitable selection of ratios. This version could consistently accelerate from a standstill to 60mph in 6.5 seconds ... a truly impressive rate of acceleration for a luxury car weighing a ton and a half. Finally, Bosch's second generation ABS braking system was adopted as standard equipment, matching braking performance with straight-line speed.

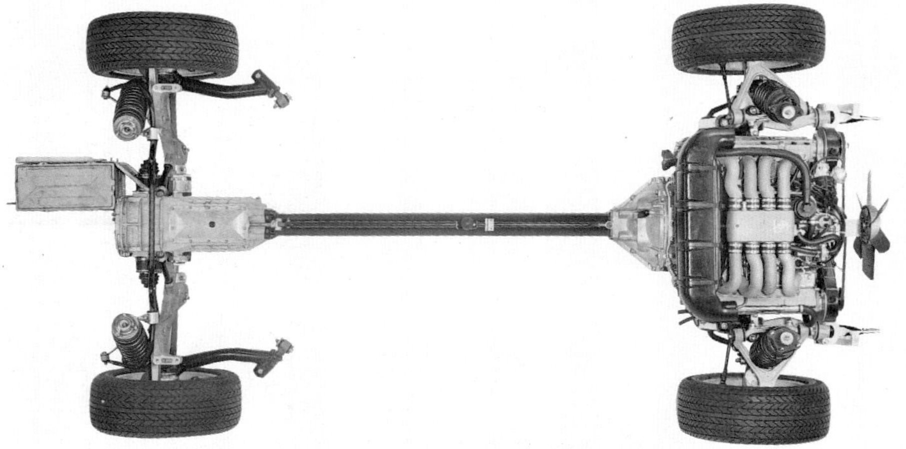

The transaxle of the Porsche 928 is similar in concept to that of the 924/944 series. A torque tube carries the prop shaft to the Porsche 5-speed manual, or Mercedes 4-speed automatic transmission. The battery is located on the back of the gearbox and dampens out all remaining vibrations.

At this time the decision was made at Weissach that all future Porsche models would have identical performance for all markets, whether or not they were equipped with catalytic converters. This policy was made politically expedient by the intention of the German authorities to switch fully to emission controls by the end of the decade, and was made possible by recent advances in micro-chip engine management controls. In future, it would be possible to determine the engine's characteristics, across a very full range of functions, simply by rewriting the microchip programmes.

In 1985 Porsche introduced the full 5-litre version of the V8 engine, with four valves per cylinder, for the American market only, raising a rather limp horsepower rating of 234bhp with catalytic equipment to a much more impressive 288bhp. Then, midway through 1986, the 32-valve 5-litre engine was released to all world markets, including America, with a power output of 320bhp.

The first series 928 engine displayed at the 1977 Geneva Show. It was progressively developed from an original capacity of 4.5 litres to a full-house 5.4 litres in the 1992 GTS. The original power output of 240bhp has risen to 340bhp, an increase of over 40% , even with the catalytic equipment installed.

Now the maximum speed was up to 168mph (faster even than the vaunted 911 Turbo), and the world was impressed.

From the 1989 model year, the 928S series 4 benefited from two technological world firsts on a production car - a tyre pressure monitoring system derived from the 959 and a self-sufficient electronic information and diagnostic system. In the Spring of 1989, the 330bhp 928GT was introduced as the sole manual representative and in the following model year both the automatic 928S series 4 and the 928GT boasted a new Porsche-developed, electronically-controlled, transverse rear differential lock-up. Known as PSD, it was based on the multi-disc lock-up first seen on the 959 and offered enhanced traction advantages as well as reducing the risk of oversteer.

Impressing the world further, Porsche introduced the new 928GTS at the beginning of 1992. Featuring a larger 5.4-litre engine, torque was increased to 500Nm at 4250rpm and power output to a maximum of 340bhp at 5700rpm. In manual form, it reached 0-100kph in 5.7 seconds and had a claimed top speed in excess of 171mph, faster than the latest 168mph 911 Turbo!

The début of the 928 at Geneva in 1977. Porsche's first eight-cylinder model was radical and innovative, with a compact water-cooled aluminium engine, advanced suspension characteristics and outstanding safety features.

PORSCHE
928

1978 brought some evolution in the internal design but little external change. This model is for export to America, having side reflectors. The deformable polyurethane front and rear body panels clothed bumper bar beams located by shock absorbers.

Originally the 928S came with the compression ratio increased from 8.1 to 10.1, and an increase in capacity to 4664cc. The result was this spoilered package with 300bhp at 5900rpm.

The rear seat of the 928 in its initial op-art upholstery. Porsche has never claimed to make a four-seater, but the back seats – which can be folded down – are fine for youngsters.

Special 'plate' wheels in forged alloy distinguished the 'S' version.

At the 1981 Geneva Show, Porsche showed the 928 PES (Porsche Experimental Structure). In case of accident the structure was reckoned by the company to be at least 50% safer for passengers and any pedestrian unlucky enough to be hit by the car.

By 1982 the 928 had undergone several minor changes under the skin but was still visibly the same car which had arrived in 1977. However, its international popularity was increasing out of all proportion to the initial reaction of the international motoring press. The 4.5-litre model was discontinued, and development concentrated on performance and efficiency.

In November 1982, Peter Lovett (GB), Gerhard Plattner (A) and Peter Zbinden (CH) took a standard 928S to the South Italian test track at Nardo. After 24 hours and a distance of 6033 kms they had achieved an average speed of 251.4kph – further and faster by 1134kms than the 956 which had won Le Mans that year.

In 1984 the 928S2 was offered with a new Daimler-Benz 4-speed automatic transmission. ABS brakes were offered as an option.

In September 1984, on Ferry Porsche's 75th birthday, the factory presented him with a longer wheelbase 928S; this was a genuine 2 + 2. The car also had a special interior, special paint and every extra the company could think of.

Prof. Porsche at the wheel of his new car, accompanied by grandson Daniel Porsche.

By 1986 the evolution had reached S4, a highly refined vehicle faster than any previous S, which handled superbly. Fully capable of cruising all day at 150mph, while returning a reasonable average consumption. The engine had by now grown to a full 5-litres as standard.

The 928S4's V8 engine, of 5-litre capacity, was uprated to 320bhp in 1986 with the help of 4-valve cylinder heads. The inlet tracts are carefully shaped to maximize the engine's torque, and to provide a ram effect for the mixture.

THE RACING LINE

When production ceased at Gmünd, in addition to the 46 aluminium-bodied cars which had found customers, the works kept a further four cars for competition and corporate use, with the spaces to run and maintain them. These cars were not only lighter than the Zuffenhausen steel-bodied cars, but they also handled and stopped better, due to their twin leading-shoe Girling brakes. In the hands of Mouche and Vueillet one of these cars took class honours in the 1951 Le Mans 24-Hour Race.

Two cars were prepared for the 1951 Liège–Rome–Liège. Both were aluminium coupés. The first (an 1100cc car), took second-in-class, driven by Huschke von Hanstein and Petermax Muller. The second carried an early series 1500 engine, winning its class and taking third overall in the hands of Guillaume and Van Der Muhle. Even so, the writing was on the wall for the cars: by 1952 the opposition had caught up and a totally new approach was needed. Short of staff and development funds, Porsche opted for a pragmatic approach. They brought in house a project started by a dealer.

Walter Glöckler, besides being the Frankfurt distributor for Porsche and VW, was a motor sports enthusiast and a fine engineer. In conjunction with his works manager he designed a small mid-engined sports racer using a modified Porsche 1100 engine and suspension carrying bodywork by Weiderhausen of Frankfurt. The car was small, agile and open-topped, in keeping with current practice. Glöckler named it Spyder and proceeded to win the 1100cc class in the German national Hillclimb Championship with Herman Kathsein – a feat duplicated in 1952 by Hans Breadal.

Having thus proved the worth of the car, Glöckler built another, this time with a 1500cc engine. This car, driven by Glöckler himself, took the 1500 class in the Hillclimb Championship in 1951 and joined the works cars for record breaking at Monthléry before being shipped over to the U.S.A. for a successful career in sports car racing.

Rallying and long distance racing formed an important part of the factory competition programme from very early days. Here a 1953 550 Spyder, road registered in Vienna, prepared for that year's Liège–Rome–Liège. With 1500cc, a dry weight of 600kg, and the racing box, the car was capable of some 225kph.

The Glöckler Spyder. Not the only Porsche special of the period but certainly the most professional. In 1100cc form it took its class in the German National Hillclimb Championship in 1951, 1952 and 1953. In 1500cc guise it showed promise and took class victory in national sports car events.

These cars were to form the basis of the legendary series of Spyders which in turn were the mainstay of Porsche competition from 1953 to 1963. The first genuine works car was a 1500cc pushrod car, débuted by Glöckler's cousin Helm, at the 1953 Eifel Sports Car Race. It took 1500cc honours from the Borgwards by a narrow margin. Two similar, although covered-cockpit, cars took the 1500cc honours by finishing abreast at that year's Le Mans 24-Hours Race, firmly establishing the 550 Spyder on its winning path.

More was to come, however, with the introduction of the type 547 engine. This 4 overhead camshaft, flat four was designed under the direction of Dr Führmann expressly for racing. It featured twin distributors, dry-sump lubrication and the latest contemporary developments in metallurgy. At its introduction it offered a useful 110bhp at 7800rpm, although the torque band was narrow and biased towards the area between 5000 and 7000rpm, confusing those drivers used to the characteristics of the old pushrod units.

In time, the engine was to grow from 1498 to 1966cc, in the process giving the company class wins and outright victories in such diverse categories as hillclimb, endurance racing, sports car racing and international Formula 2. At its first attempt, the combination of 550 Spyder and 547 engine took Hans Herrman and Herbert Linge to 1500cc class victory and a resounding sixth overall in the Mille Miglia, while at Le Mans a single survivor took the class after running the final four hours on three cylinders.

In common with the boxer configuration, another feature of the Glöckler car which was to survive into the 1960s was the tubular frame construction. As the Spyders progressed from the 550 to 550A, the RSK1500, the RS60 and RS61, the tubular frame with aluminium skin remained. Under the skin, however, the cars became increasingly sophisticated. One feature of all the Spyders, and the descendant 904, was that they could also be used as fast road cars by those who wanted the best in handling, response and engineering excellence – and were willing to pay for it.

Chronology

1950
Glöckler Spyder, a ladder-type chassis, VW gearbox and a 1086cc Porsche engine mid-mounted produced max 58bhp on racing fuel.

1951
Glöckler Sypder. As above but with 1498cc engine.

1953
The type 550, introduced with 1500cc pushrod engine from the Super. Suspension was similar to the road cars. Both coupés and open cars were built.

1954
The 547 engine was introduced, offering 110bhp at 7800rpm. Dual coils and ignition from the start. Chassis nos. 550001–015.

1955
Porsche 5-speed gearbox débuted at the Tourist Trophy, although type number remained 550. Chassis nos. 550016–090.

1956
550A was announced, with space-frame construction and all round improvements in weight-saving and aerodynamics; 135bhp at 7200rpm. Chassis nos. 550A 1010–104, 0110–0113 also 0131.

1957
Detail refinements. Chassis nos. 550A 0114–0144.

1958
718 series adopted, known as 1500RSK due to suspension layout, and later abandoned. 547/3 engine gave a 148bhp at 8000rpm in normal tune, 142bhp at 7500rpm with Le Mans tune and gearing. Chassis nos 718–001 to 718–034.

1959
718 RS60, similar to 1500RSK, with detailed body modifications to meet FIA regulations. Three stages of engine development; 547/3/4/5 gave 150, 160 and 180bhp respectively. Chassis nos. 718051–718064.

1960
RS61, basically similar to RS60, except in detail. Chassis nos.718065–718078.

A 1955, 1500RS (chassis number 5500057) now in private hands. Note the brake-cooling ducts, modified front cover and faired-in headlamps. Nonetheless, with the exception of the head fairing, the car still bears a remarkable resemblance to the 1955 356.

1961
RS61 Le Mans. Eventually developed 185bhp at 7200rpm. Chassis nos. 718044–045. Also Chassis nos. 718046–047 with eight-cylinder engines offering 210bhp at 8400rpm. Known as GTR.

1962
046–047 appear as Spyders for hillclimbs, known only as 718. Capable of 270bhp at 8600rpm.

Porsche historian and works driver, Richard von Frankenberg, pictured ready for the start at Spa, 1956. The car looks extremely standard with its white steering wheel and dials from the road-going 356.

Von Frankenberg at speed in the 1957 Nürburgring 1000 kilometres race. The factory claim 38 of these 550A 1500RS Spyders were built.

The last 550A 1500RS. Richard Von Frankenberg raced the car only once before it was sold to long-time Porsche enthusiast and famous conductor Herbert von Karajan for road use.

A 550A 1500RS at speed in the 1958 San Salvador Grand Prix. Note the general lack of crowd protection, a feature of road races in the 1950s.

The European Hillclimb Championship at Ollon-Villars 1958. The whole works team were present, including Hans Herrmann, Edgar Barth, Ernest Vogel and Heini Walter.

Ollon-Villars 1958 again. Wolfgang Graf Berghe (Taffy) von Trips at speed in the RSK Spyder, apparently recovering from an earlier excursion!

Spa Francorchamps May 1959. Bino Heins at the wheel of a 550RSK, leaving the paddock.

The 1959 RS60. Apart from the full-height windscreen and a luggage compartment in keeping with Le Mans regulations, the main differences from the RSK1500 were in aerodynamics and weight distribution. The wheelbase was increased by 100mm and the length by 10mm. Originally introduced with 150bhp at 7800rpm from a 1587cc engine, development yielded 160bhp in 1960 and 180bhp in 1961, at the same engine speed.

Manfred Jantke and Huschke von Hanstein, former public relations managers, confer at the Nürburgring anniversary meeting in 1976. The car is the RS60 from the Porsche museum.

Jean Behra, in the car, with co-driver Edgar Barth, prior to the start of the Goodwood meeting in September 1958. The car is a 550RSK. Note the lack of rear fairing for the driver, also the lack of roll-over protection.

The RS61 offered a revised rear suspension system with twin rear wishbones and radius rod lower location. The wheelbase was the same as the RS60, as were the track and overall length. Weight was increased by 40kg (590 as opposed to 550). This car with its modified roof ran at Le Mans in 1961 in the prototype class. It was the first car to be equipped with the parallel action wiper, a feature of all the later Porsche racing coupés, although as seen here it carried the normal article.

An RS61. Never raced or rallied, this particular example was used as a road-car by its original owner!

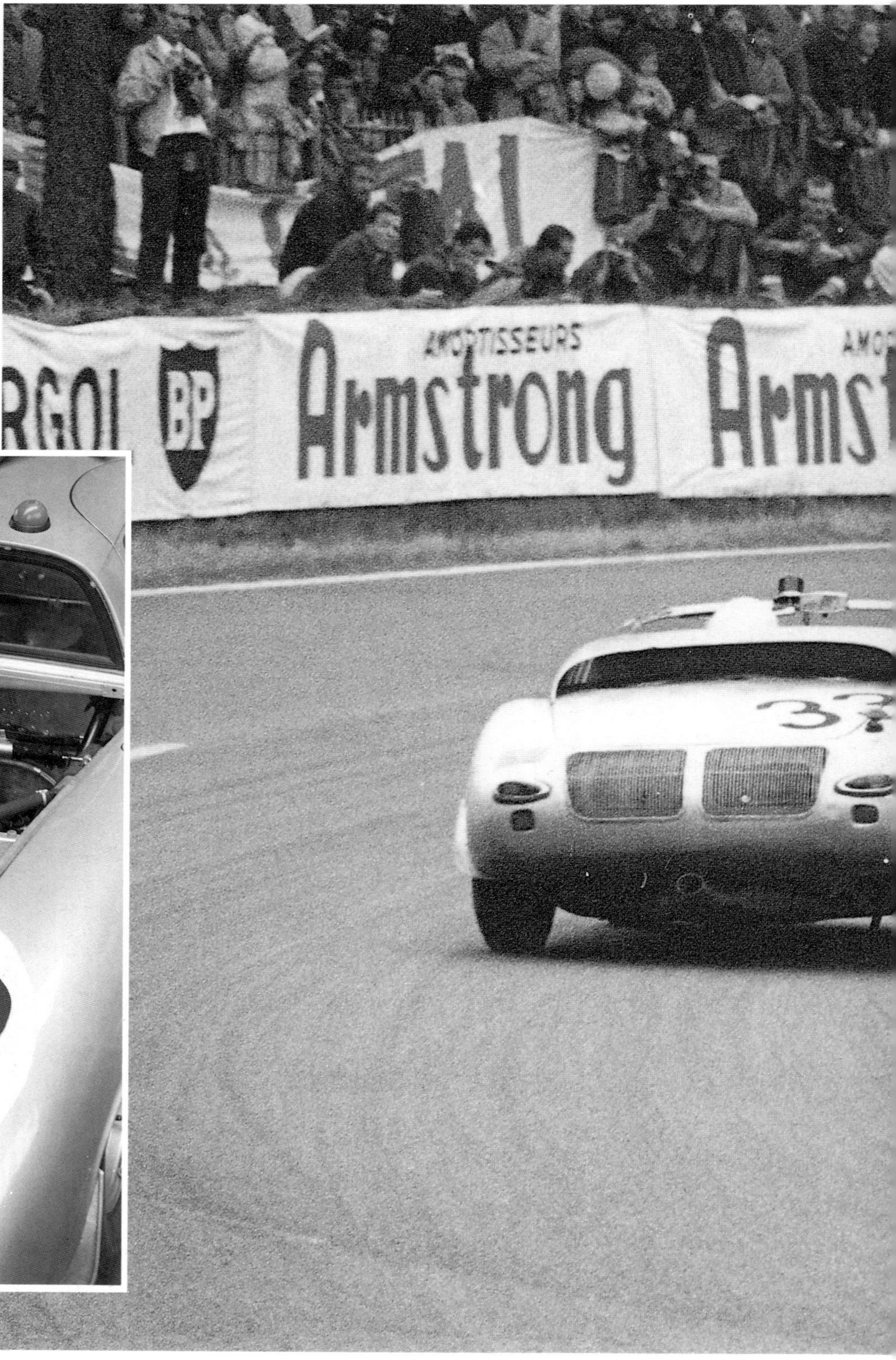

The four-cylinder 'Führmann' engine of the RS61. This example is a closed Le Mans specification car.

The Gregory-Holbert RS61 on its way to fifth overall in the 1961 Le Mans 24-Hour race. This was a Targa-type body. Five works cars competed, three finished. While number 33 carried a 1967cc engine (chassis no.18-047), number 32, driven by Barth and Herrmann, used a 1600cc unit, finishing seventh overall and second in class (chassis no. 718-045).

Herbert Müller demonstrates the RS61 Bergspyder nicknamed 'grandmother' after taking Edgar Barth to the European Hillclimb Championships in 1963 and 1964.

The works team used BP to win the 1963 Targa Florio. The winning car was number 142, driven by Bonnier and Abate. In the foreground, an eight-cylinder RS61 Spyder, without the usual factory driving lights, entered for Maglioli and Baghetti.

THE 904 TO 910

By the early 1960s, the smaller classes of international sports car racing had become the domain of the specialist chassis-builder, while competition in the larger classes languished after Aston Martin gave up the expensive struggle against Ferrari. Only the GT class offered Porsche a realistic ratio of success to investment and towards this end, in 1963, a totally new car was developed – the 904.

From the outset the 904 was seen as a multi-purpose vehicle, a fast road car, a possible rally contender, and, with six or eight cylinders fitted, a contender for GT or overall honours in endurance racing. Porsche unashamedly adopted the latest in chassis and body technology of their rivals. The result was a super, strong, lightweight GRP monocoque carrying the mechanical and suspension components on a rectangular section pressed-steel subframe which was bonded to the body.

A further break with tradition was the adoption of unequal-length wishbones front and rear, with coils over shocks located by forward-reaching radius arms. This suspension was to carry over almost unchanged to the 906 and influence all succeeding race cars to some extent. The steering was adjustable, as were the seat and pedal positions, and further bushed to counter aggressive kickback. With all the fuel carried in the front, the balance of this lightweight was subject to considerable variance: 48/52 front to rear with full tanks, 42/58 dry. Nonetheless the car was popular with its drivers and coped well with adverse conditions, as demonstrated by Bohringer and Wutherich – taking second overall in the 1965 Monte Carlo Rally in wintery conditions.

Although planned for a limited series of 100 cars, at least 120 were laid down of which 116 were sold. Initially the cars were supplied only with the 547 series engine offering 180bhp at 7800rpm or 155bhp at 6900rpm in road trim. Later at least ten examples of the 904/6 were constructed, some reconverted from 904/8 configuration. With this in mind it is probably fair to assume that all the chassis numbers form 904 001 to 904 116 were built up, numbers 117–20 being used as factory spares. Thus numbers 001–006 and 113–6 could have been 904/6 or 904/8 configurations at some time. This however, is hypothesis, for the factory lists only 007–16 as 904 or Carrera GTS, with 001–006 as 904/6 or 904/8 spec. cars.

With the 904 established as a front runner in the GT class and a full order book, Porsche could well have built and sold more, or chosen to develop the car further. However, the 1966 regulations opened up a whole new category for Sports Cars having an annual production run of 50 units, and a new venture was launched. In view of the unreliability of the eight-cylinder in the 904/8, the decision was taken to concentrate in the short term on the racing variant of the 901 engine for endurance events. To this end a space-frame car, using the suspension of the 904 and a completely new GRP bodyshell, was developed. This was the 906.

Customer demand was such that even though the car proved impossible to homologate for road use, some 65 units, excepting pre-production prototypes, were built. For official purposes the factory called the cars Carrera 6s. Regardless of this, as with the 904, the public chose to adopt the type number for the car.

At only one metre high, and styled more by the wind tunnel than the stylists, the 906 caused a sensation. The design incorporated lessons learned by the factory from its experience with the light and ingenious Elva-Porsche, campaigned in

1964 and 1965 by Müller, and in its suspension and geometry owed much to the purchase by the factory of a complete set of uprights, hub assemblies and wheels from the Lotus Formula 1 team.

On its first showing, in the 1966 Daytona 24-Hour Race, the new car took sixth overall and first in the 2-litre prototype class. It went on to achieve success in the U.S.A. and Europe, staying competitive until a new generation of Chevrons and Lolas arrived to claim the class as their own. In its evolution, the 906 was offered with Weber carburation and Bosch fuel injection on the six-cylinder cars, while the type 771 eight-cylinder unit finally found reliability in the chassis. More importantly, perhaps, it introduced a new era of ultra-light space-frames to the company, in the process becoming the first Porsche to make use of titanium.

Apart from the 906, the 910 owed its existence to the lessons learned from the Elva-Porsche and the Lotus components in the 1965 Hillclimb car. By 1968 the car was a mobile test bed of exotic metals, including titanium and aluminium space-frame components and magnesium engine castings. Apart from the development 910 Bergspyders, some 28 cars were built, a fact which automatically homologated the car as a Sports Car when the FIA regulations for 1968 were finalized.

Using both the six- and eight-cylinder engines, the 910 was an extremely sophisticated machine offering superior aerodynamics to the 906, plus a substantial saving in weight. It was also a far more expensive car to produce – which did not deter the factory from developing it into the 907, the first factory racer with right-hand drive.

The 907 featured variable spring ratios, developed originally on the works' long-distance 910s. Also, the aerodynamics were cleaner than either the 906 or the 910. Some 20 cars were built in this series, 16 with eight-cylinder engines and, to ensure reliability, four with six-cylinder engines for Le Mans. The 907 ran only in the prototype category in 1967 and 1968, while the main opposition came from the John Wyer-entered GT40s.

Another direct development of the 910, albeit not as successful as the 907, was the 909 Bergspyder. Two of these cars were built, the main difference from the 910 being the mounting of the gearbox in front of the rear axle. In early showings the cars were sidelined by fuel delivery problems, nonetheless valuable practical experience was gained from these.

At the Le Mans qualifying meeting in April 1968, two modified long-tailed 908s were entered. Bearing the chassis numbers 908001 and 002, they contained Porsche's answer to the 1968 FIA regulations allowing prototypes of up to 3 litres: the Hans Mezger-designed 2997cc flat 8 engine which, in various forms, was to remain competitive into the early 1980s.

With heads and barrels of aluminium, a magnesium crankcase and titanium con rods and bolts, the engine was an expensive exercise in metallurgy. The resulting unit weighed only 393lbs and in works' cars was offering 310bhp at 8000rpm at the first outing at Monza in 1968. Later engines were reputed to give up to 370bhp at 8500rpm, but the factory stuck to the more modest claim of 350bhp at 8400.

With four overhead cams acting on twin, sodium-filled valves, the engine became one of the most reliable units the factory ever produced. With the 908, Porsche clinched the World Manufacturers' Championships for the first time in

1969, finally breaking the Ford domination which the 907 had come close to disturbing in 1967, and opening the way for a succession of wins with the car which included eleven outright championship victories over the four seasons from 1968 to 1972. Perhaps unfairly, however, the 908 was to be overshadowed by one of the greatest racing cars ever built – the fearsome 917.

The glass-fibre monocoque and rear subframe of the 904. The body was fabricated by the Heinkel aviation works in Speyr.

Body and subframe of the 904 weighed only about 320lbs. Styling was an example of Butzi Porsche's finest work.

The 940 GTS prototype. By the start of 1964 over 100 examples had been ordered by private customers.

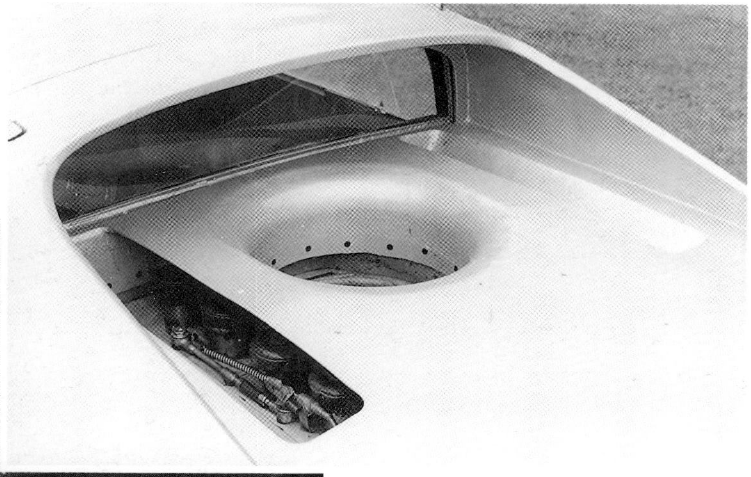

The rear deck of the 904/8 gave notice of future Porsche practice, as can be seen from this shot of the 1965 prototype.

'What looks right usually is right', is an adage often heard in motor racing. Somehow the 771 engine looks out of place in the 904.

The 1964 Targa Florio was won by the production 904 of Colin Davis and Antonio Pucci. Here the 904/8 of Bonnier and Hill contests the 1965 race, which was won by Ferrari, with Davis and Mitter second in a 904/8 Spyder.

Possibly the most beautiful of all Porsche racing cars, the 904 at speed in the hands of Herbert Linge–Gerhard Mitter at the Nürburgring 1000 Kilometres in 1964.

Herbert Müller in the 1964 Nürburgring 1000 Kilometres race (car no.55), and at Le Mans the same year in the Scuderia Fillipinetti 904. Six- and eight-cylinder 904s shared the same shell; this car was a 904/6.

The only eight-cylinder 904 at Le Mans in 1965. Disappointingly, it failed to finish due to an early clutch failure. Drivers were Davis and Mitter.

In 1964 Porsche commissioned a rolling chassis from the British manufacturer Elva. This was fitted with an eight-cylinder engine, and, although used for research and development purposes, was campaigned in the 1965 European Hillclimb Championship. Here the car is seen at Trento-Bondone with Herbert Müller at the wheel.

With specialist chassis manufacturers beginning to encroach on the territory Porsche regarded as its own, the 906 was a quantum leap in style and component packaging. Influenced by both Lotus and Elva, the company created a really sleek machine under the direction of Dr Ferdinand Piëch.

The 906, or Carrera 6, was available with a choice of six- or eight-cylinder engines. In its first year a six-cylinder car captured the index of performance at Le Mans. The customer cars were supplied on steel wheels, a carry-over from the 904 programme.

Schauinsland 1966. A 906 is put through its paces. The use of stabilizing flaps on the front bodywork is quite new.

The 906 LH (long-tail). The weight penalty of the tail was supposedly offset by the superior drag co-efficient of the extra length. With these cars and subsequent 907s, 908s and early 917s, the penalty was an imprecise high-speed handling. Two works' prototypes undergo tests at Hockenheim prior to Le Mans in 1966.

The six-cylinder engine in the 906.

The fifth-placed 906 (chassis no. 143) long-tail of Hans Herrmann and Herbert Linge at its pit in the 1966 Le Mans 24-Hour race.

Car no. 37 at the 1967 Le Mans 24-Hour race was this 906 driven by Vic Elford and Ben Pon. It was placed seventh overall and won the Sports Category.

A six-cylinder installation in a 906 for the 1968 Le Mans 24-Hour race.

The 910, introduced in 1967, had a 2-litre, six-cylinder engine in customer form or a flat 8, used by the works. This is a six-cylinder car, chassis no.910-007.

910-007 at Le Mans in 1968, where it retired after 23 hours.

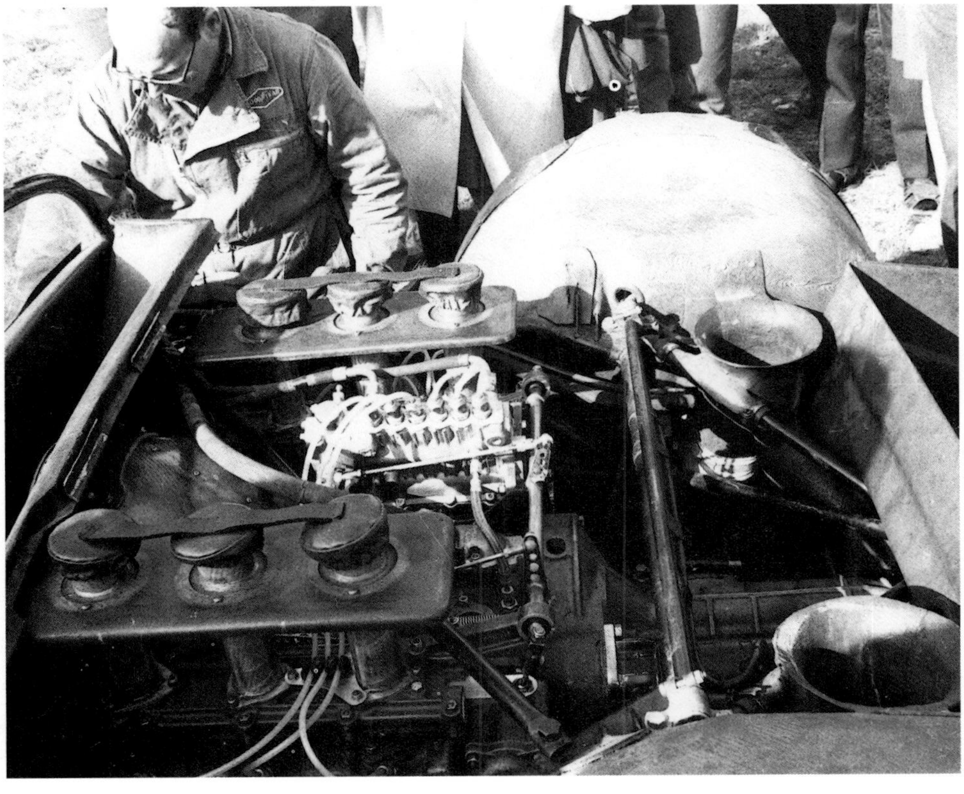

The engine installation in 910-007. In long-distance form the output was 220bhp at 8000rpm. Note the complex fuel injection.

Rolf Stommelen in the 910 Bergspyder. Campaigned by the works in 1967-8, the fully developed weight was just 882lbs. The 910 took Gerhard Mitter the European Hillclimb Championship in 1967 and 1968.

A factory 910 eight-cylinder, at the Nürburgring 1976.

With the 907, Porsche made use of improved aerodynamics.

In 1968 Porsche came close to winning Le Mans with this 907 driven by Spoerry and Steinemann. The car finished second overall, third in the index of performance and won the Sports-Prototype class.

The spartan interior of the Wicky Racing 907.

Gerhard Mitter shared this 907 with the immortal Jo Siffert in the 1968 Daytona 24-Hour race. They finished a creditable second.

This 907 long-tail, with an eight-cylinder engine, failed to make the distance at Le Mans in 1968.

52
P
PORSCHE

A 907 with a six-cylinder engine. Unfortunately the whole of 1968 was disastrous, as the works struggled to sort the new 908s. This is the Nürburgring in 1968. From 1969, the 908 won the 1000 Kilometres race three years running.

The 907 long-tail of Alex Soler-Roig and Rudi Lins prior to the start of the 1968 Le Mans 24-Hour race. The long-tail was to maximize aerodynamic efficiency on the long straights. The engineer on the left is Professor Helmuth Bott, Porsche Director of Research and Development from 1972 - 1988.

One of the factory 908s on its first Le Mans outing in 1968. This example (chassis no. 908-015), complete with primitive spoiler, was handled by Joe Buzzetta and Scooter Patrick. It retired early in the race.

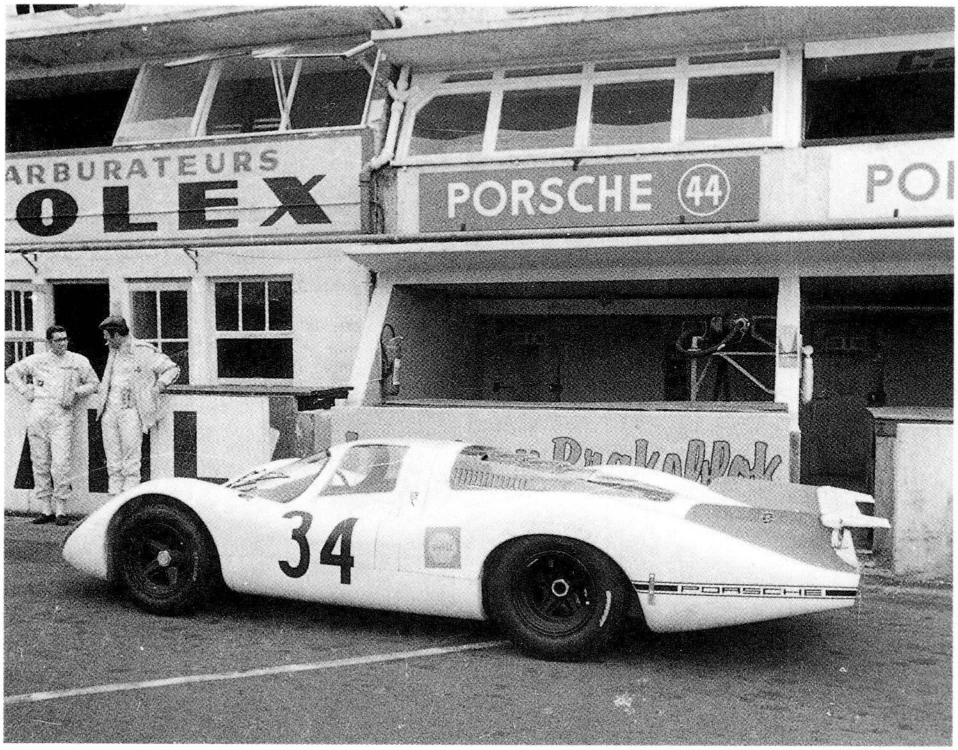

Hans Herrmann and Gerard Larrousse took this long-tailed 908 to second overall in the 1969 Le Mans 24-Hours (chassis no. 908-031).

Le Mans 1969 was one of the closest ever, Ickx in the GT40 finishing just two seconds ahead of Herrmann in the 908. Here Herrmann relieves Gérard Larrousse for the final stint.

By 1970 the Porsche-Martini link had been securely forged by the Austrian operation. This is the Rudi Lins–Helmut Marko car, chassis no. 908-050 at Le Mans scrutineering.

The Lins–Marko car on its way to third overall at Le Mans 1970. It took first in the Sports-Prototype class and the index of performance.

The 908/2 made its début in 1969. Nicknamed Sole (as in flatfish) by the works, it had a higher waistline and more enveloping shape than the early cars. Stabilizing tabs were used at the front as aerofoils were no longer permitted.

Porsche produced the 908/3 specifically for the Nürburgring and Targa Florio. It shows the contemporary influence of Chevron and Lola in the bodystyle. This, the Scuderia Montjuich car, failed to finish in the 1972 Le Mans 24-Hour race.

Although thoroughly outclassed, Joest, Weber and Casoni drove this 908 into third overall at the 1972 Le Mans 24 Hours. The previous owner was Jo Siffert.

Interserie champion Leo Kinnunen and Herbert Müller brought this 908 turbo into third place at the 1975 Nürburgring 1000 Kilometres.

FINA
TUDOR
FINA
Marlboro
35

Herbert Müller

THE 917

The 917 was something special. It gave Porsche their first Le Mans win in 1970, and dominated the whole sports car racing world wherever it ran. This legend will no doubt give Porsche their first million-dollar classic car sale.

No-one who ever heard a 917 out for blood, let alone saw Vic Elford, Pedro Rodriguez or Jo Siffert hauling the brutes round bends which were once thought only mildly spectacular, can forget them.

True, the record of wins was helped by Ferrari's over-commitment to Formula One and reluctance to embrace the type of almost unproven talent which the customer teams let loose in the 917. Even so, the 917 ranks with the W125 Mercedes or the Lotus 72 among the exceptionally great racing cars.

The car was sensational from the word go. Twenty-five were lined up outside the factory in 1969 to prove homologation. The curvaceous beast was at the 1969 Geneva Show with suspension-operated trim tabs and a flat 12 engine of 4494cc, with a central drive take off which already delivered a healthy 542bhp. All for a modest DM140,000.

Yet it was a pig in its early form. Its handling gave even the finest drivers hairy moments. Only when John Wyer stepped in, having brought both Aston Martin and the Ford GT40 to success, did the car begin to show its true mettle.

While the factory had been trying to stop the ill-handling by constant chassis development, David Yorke and John Horsman of J.W. Automotive found solutions by working with aerodynamics.

This heavily airbrushed rear view was one of the photographs with which Porsche introduced the legendary 917. The car arrived in response to the 1968 FIA Group 4 regulations for sports cars with a minimum production of 25 in a year. Upon introduction, the factory claimed 520bhp from the air-cooled 4.5-litre flat 12 engine, with 320kph attainable on the Mulsanne straight. The car was also shown at the Geneva Show in March 1969 and the homologation run of 25 was ready by 21 April for acceptance by 1 May. In flamboyant style the factory lined up all 25 examples outside the Zuffenhausen works and invited FIA representative Dean Delamont to drive any one of them.

Long-tailed (LH), short-tailed (K) and Can-Am type cars were built from 1970 on. The engine grew from its original 4490cc through 4907cc, 4998cc, to a full house 5374cc.

By 1972 it had been outlawed by the CSI for World Championship events. The emphasis immediately switched to Can-Am , hitherto dominated by the fabulous Gulf McLarens.

For this a 4998cc engine (later the 5.4-litre), already proven in European Inter-Series racing, was used with twin turbochargers. The resulting 1100bhp, and the Middle East War, spelled the end of Can-Am. When the engines made a brief appearance in the Inter-Series, that too ended in disarray. By 1974 the 917 was no more.

The epitaph of the 917 lies in the memory of those who heard and saw, even felt, them racing and in the vast amounts they fetch from collectors. All in all, it was the car which finally put Porsche on a par with any other world-class racing manufacturer.

Perhaps the epitome of the 917 arrived with the 1973 Can-Am Spyder. With its 1100bhp it could hurl itself through the 100mph mark in 3 seconds, the 200mph barrier in 13 seconds and unofficially the top speed was calculated at a staggering 260mph plus. A closed-circuit speed record of 221mph for nearly 15 years in the hands of Mark Donohue at Talladega Speedway really tells its own story.

Le Mans 1969. Car number 14, the Stommelen-Ahrens car (chassis no. 917-007). It retired at half distance and was later sold to the U.S.A. Early in the race the British driver John Woolfe was killed when his privately-owned 917 (believed to be chassis no. 917-005) crashed.

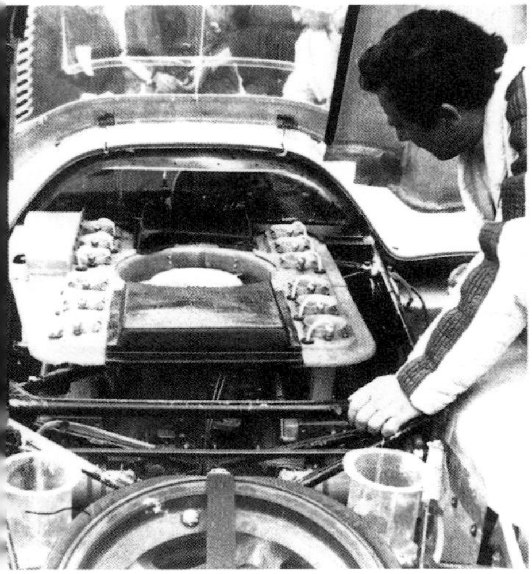

The engine room of the 917. This shot clearly shows the space-saver tyre.

Car number 12 (chassis no.008) was the Vic Elford–Richard Attwood long-tail. This car showed its potential by leading healthily until forced to retire by clutch failure at 21 hours.

Jo Siffert gained an overall fourth place in the 1969 Can-Am Series with this 917 PA Spyder. The PA stood for Porsche–Audi, the U.S. distributors who were the entrants and principal sponsors of the car. Note the suspension-operated rear trim tabs, a feature soon made redundant on the endurance racers.

Run by Porsche–Salzburg, the 917 driven by Hans Herrmann and Richard Attwood (chassis no. 917-023) gave Porsche their first overall victory at Le Mans in 1970. The car was later sold into private ownership in the U.S.A. These cars became known as the 917K, for Kurz (short-tail).

From the end of the 1969 season the factory effort with the 917 was handled by the John Wyer organization. This was the only team to deal direct with the works, all the others were serviced through the sports service department rather than the experimental divisions. Here Leo Kinnunen is seen beside the car (chassis no.015) which he took to victory, in company with Pedro Rodriguez, in the Daytona 24-Hour race in 1970.

Car number 24 was entered for the 1970 Le Mans 24-Hour race to be driven by Steinemann and Spoerry. It did not feature in the race, functioning as a back-up car.

The Porsche Salzburg cars had a green and purple psychedelic paint job for 1970. This is the 917K (chassis no. 917-014) of Gijs Van Lennep and Gérard Larrousse which came ninth overall at the Watkins Glen Race in 1970. The car following is the Ferrari 512S of Mario Andretti while the Porsche–Audi 917 of Vic Elford and Denny Hulme brings up the rear.

1970 was a bad year for the Gulf JW team at Le Mans. Car number 21 (chassis no. 917-044) was retired fairly early on by Rodriguez and Kinnunen. The second car (chassis no. 917-043) was just unable to make the half distance driven by Jo Siffert and Brian Redman. The car wearing race number 20 had the new 4.9-litre engine which suffered a 'teething malfunction'.

The ultimate long-distance 917 was this JW example with fins and aerofoil, developed specifically for Le Mans 1971. The example shown here on display at the 1972 Geneva Show retired when running in sixth place. (chassis no. 917-045).

Siffert and Bell took this 917K (chassis no. 029) to victory in the 1971 Buenos-Aires 1000 Kilometres. This was this particular car's first race. Derek Bell is holding his helmet to the left of the picture as Seppi climbs into the car. On the right is David Yorke.

A weary Pedro Rodriguez shares victory in the 1971 Daytona 24-Hour race with his pit crew.

When the design office at Porsche were given a free hand to decorate a 917 they created this tongue-in-cheek livery. The 'Schwein', or 'The Pink Pig' as English speakers called it, closely resembled a butcher's cutting chart, neatly rendered in porcine pink! The car ran at Le Mans in 1971 and was designated the 917/20, a unique car. In essence, the voluminous curves were an attempt by the SERA Organization design studios to get a better drag coefficient without a full long-tailed body. In the race, Reinhold Joest crashed heavily, putting the car out on Sunday morning.

The 917LH, handled by Vic Elford and Gérard Larrousse in the 1971 Le Mans 24-Hour race. It retired before half distance when the cooling mounting bolts sheared, causing a panic in the Martini pits. The winning car was a Martini 917K, handled by Van Lennep and Marko, which also had trouble with cooling and alternator drive belts.

The drilled and ventilated disc brakes of the 917 were to become the standard wear of a whole generation of Porsche racers, right up to the 936.

With the 917-10 the 917 started on the way to engine outputs of 1000+bhp via turbocharging. The installation was neat and functional. Only the boost gauge differed in the cockpit.

With long-distance racing closed to it, the 917 was reduced to Group 7 and Interserie. Here Herbert Müller is seen at the wheel of a 4.5-litre turbo 917-10. The cars were run by Willi Kauhsen for the Martini–Porsche team in 1971 and 1972.

The system, designed by Ing Hans Mezger and productionized by Valentin Schäfer used a large KKK turbocharger made by Eberspacher.

The 908/03 model had a new lease of life when the 2.1-litre turbo engine was installed for endurance racing. Here Herbert Müller takes over from Gijs Van Lennep in the 1975 Dijon 1000 Kilometres.

When George Follmer stood in for the injured Mark Donohue in the 1972 Penske campaign in the Can-Am series, he achieved instant success. The following year Bobby Rinzler bought chassis nos. 917-10-003 and 005 for him to contest the 1973 series. He also took in some Interserie rounds, such as the one at the Nürburgring.

Having bought 917/10-002 from the factory, Jo Siffert proceeded to scrape up enough backing to run the car privately in the 1971 Can-Am series. He was standing fourth in the championship at the time of his fatal accident at Brands Hatch. He is seen here with his two devoted mechanics, Edi Wyss and Hugo Shibler.

A rule change meant that the 917 would once again be eligible for Le Mans. Using factory-supplied drawings, the Kremer brothers built this one. Lack of testing and the rise in efficiency of the turbocharged opposition effectively killed the project.

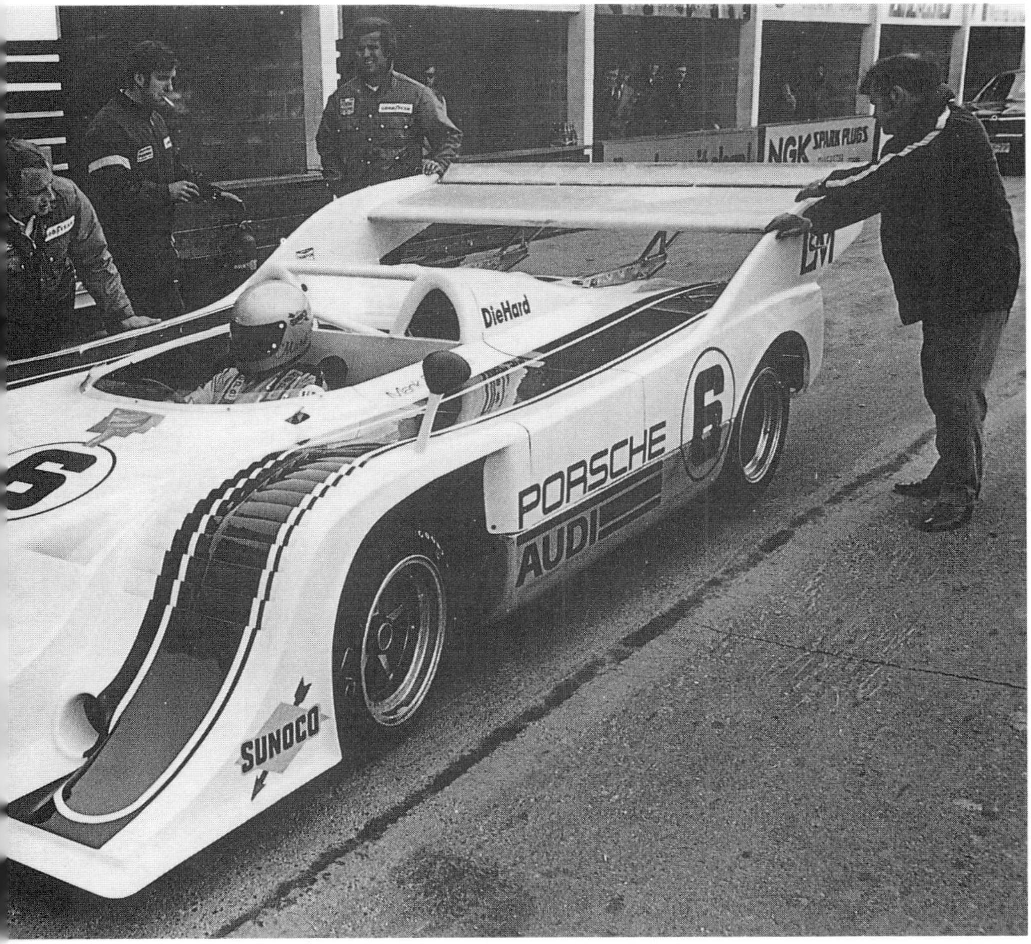

Three 917-30 series cars were built. The first 917-30-001 was retained by the works and later converted back to 917-10 specification except for various body panels. The second two, 002 and 003, went to Roger Penske for Mark Donohue. The turbocharged 5347cc engine gave up to 1100bhp at 7800rpm with full boost, and was at that time the world's most powerful road racing car. The body was designed to create enormous downforce: to lift off the accelerator was like hitting the brake pedal in another racing car, said Brian Redman.

THE TURBO ERA — 936 TO 962

Engineers Mezger and Schäfer mastered the difficult techniques of turbocharging racing engines in the 1972–1973 period (in particular, wastegate control was improved substantially, to reduce the 'turbo lag' phenomenon that drivers complained of), and as we've related in another chapter, the roadgoing 911 Turbo was the first to benefit.

Following the cancellation of the Can-Am programme at the end of 1973, work began at once on applying a single turbo to the 911 model, which became the 911 Carrera Turbo for competition purposes. It could only have a 2.1-litre capacity engine, so that when the FIA's equivalency factor of 1.4 was applied (to a supercharged, or equivalent engine) the capacity would not exceed the mandatory 3.0-litre capacity, but still the power was quoted at between 450 and 500 horsepower, depending on how much boost pressure was applied. (At that time the 911 Carrera 3.0 RSR was delivering 330bhp without turbocharging, so the power rose by up to 50% from an engine which was some 70% of the capacity).

The turbo prototype finished second at Le Mans in 1974, and with all the lessons learned Porsche withdrew from the 1975 racing season to prepare for 1976, when an entirely new set of regulations would be introduced for Group 4 grand touring cars, Group 5 (Silhouette) cars for the World Championship for Manufacturers, and - announced only towards the end of 1975 - a Group 6 sports racing car category, the one we concentrate upon in this chapter.

It was a brilliant era for Porsche, a period in which all the ground lost to SEFAC Ferrari in the 1950s was regained. But the Italian manufacturer was absent, concentrating fully upon Formula 1 racing, and for all of Porsche's success there was usually a feeling that no worthy opponent had presented itself.

Porsche won all three major championships in 1976. Customers were almost unopposed in the European Grand Touring Car Championship, in which the 3-litre 934 model was a giant. The Martini–Porsche factory team had a nasty mid-season scare with the 935 models, the specification of which had to be altered very hurriedly following a clarification from the FIA, but eventually the challenge from BMW was conquered. In Group 6, Porsche won the World Sports Car Championship handsomely from Renault–Alpine, despite running a single car for Jacky Ickx and Jochen Mass against two, sometimes three, from the French manufacturer. And best of all, the 936 of Ickx and Gijs van Lennep won the Le Mans 24-Hour race with ease, Porsche's third major success at the Sarthe.

In 1977 a degree of boredom crept in, which was a pity. Customers still ruled the roost in Group 4, and the Martini works team, and customers, fought between themselves for the spoils in Group 5 World Championship. There was no effective competition at all. In Group 6, neither Porsche nor Renault–Alpine chose to do the full series, which was dominated by Alfa Romeo, but they slugged out a super contest at Le Mans, which Alfa did not include in its programme. Again, it was Porsche's victory at the Sarthe.

In 1978 Porsche left its customers to take charge of the World Championship for Manufacturers (an ironic situation), but paused to produce the superb 935/78 model which took the Group 5 Silhouette regulations to the very boundary of credibility, and crushed all opposition at Silverstone. The 3.2-litre engine, with water-cooled cylinder heads, developed an easy 750bhp and raised the technological level to a new peak. But still, the engine misbehaved at Le Mans,

For 1976, Porsche decided to contest the World Sports Car Championships in Group 6. For this purpose two 936s were constructed using an amalgamation of 908-3 and 917-10 components and featuring a 2140cc turbocharged flat 6 engine, giving 520bhp at 8000rpm. Later, at least one more of these Spyders was built. However, chassis nos. 936-001 and 002 were constantly updated, retiring only after the 1981 season. Here Jacky Ickx confers with co-driver Gijs Van Lennep at practice for the 1976 Le Mans 24-Hour race, which they duly won.

and the 935/78 was then put away in the Porsche museum. The 1978 race was won, deservedly, by Renault–Alpine, with Porsches second and third, and with that the French manufacturer withdrew to concentrate on its Grand Prix development.

The Group 6 sports car championship fizzled out in 1978, and the Group 4 championship soon followed. Group 5 was kept alive until the end of 1981, when it could be given a decent burial, with an epitaph describing how Porsche, and its customers, had become the victim of its own success. The marque was *so* good at its job that it had no realistic competition.

Lancia, in fact, won the Manufacturers' Championship in 1980 and in 1981, simply by winning the 2-litre division with 1.4-litre, turbocharged sports cars, thinly disguised Monte Carlo production models. In the meantime, Kremer Porsche Racing won at Le Mans in 1979 with a Porsche 935, and the Porsche factory returned to the rostrum in 1981 with a much developed 936 model driven by Jacky Ickx and Derek Bell.

Perhaps the new Group C World Endurance Championship, introduced in 1982, would be a different story. Any manufacturer could compete, with any type of engine; all that was required was a fuel consumption not exceeding 600 litres per 1000 kilometres, or pro rata for distance. Ford tried hard with the new C100 model, powered by a Cosworth V8 engine, and the make had a number of

Le Mans 1977. The Ickx/van Lennep 936 on its way to victory for the second year running, and at its triumphant civic reception in Stuttgart. Incorporating features of both the 908/3 and the 917/10, the 936 used a similar six-cylinder engine to the 935 and raced in Group 6. The 936 model earned Porsche's third Le Mans victory in 1976, and won the 24-Hour race again in 1977 and finally in 1981. Latterly the engine was 2.65 litres in capacity and developed 650bhp.

customers. Lancia tried hard, and so did specialist makes such as Aston Martin, but once again Porsche produced the ultimate weapon, the 956 model, powered (as the 936 had been the year before) by a 2.65-litre flat-six engine with four valves per cylinder.

The 956 proved to be the best in the field, winning every race it contested in 1982. Three factory cars, sponsored by Rothmans, took the top three places at Le Mans, and when Porsche released a dozen replicas to customers for the 1983 season, rival makes realized that it would take a miracle to change the pattern of history.

Lancia tried valiantly, from 1983 to the end of 1985, but beat the factory Porsches only once, at Spa in 1985, and then in sad circumstances. The race was stopped prematurely following the death of Stefan Bellof, one of Porsche's star drivers.

Eventually though, opposition did come, from Jaguar and from Mercedes. Porsche stayed faithful to the 962 model which succeeded the 956, and wrung the last ounce of development out of it in 1987. Porsche won Le Mans again, for the seventh year in succession in 1987, but Jaguar won the World Sports-Prototype Championship (as the series was now named). Unless Porsche built a new car, and there was no sign of that happening while it prepared to contest the American single-seater CART series, it could offer no greater resistance.

Finally, Jaguar beat Porsche at Le Mans in 1988, but the margin over the Derek Bell/Hans Stuck/Klaus Ludwig Porsche 962C which put up a fighting finish was merely 2½ minutes. And then Jaguar itself came under extreme pressure from Sauber–Mercedes ...

On behalf of the Arabian TAG consortium, Porsche designed, developed and prepared the 1.6-litre, turbocharged V6 engines that powered the Marlboro McLaren team, and Niki Lauda and Alain Prost, to three consecutive World Formula 1 Championships between 1984 and 1986. The contract expired at the end of 1987 and then Porsche, in its own right, tackled the specialized world of CART single-seater racing. Hans Mezger and Valentin Schäfer were again responsible for engine design, while the Porsche sports car chassis designer Horst Reitter designed the composite materials monocoque. The car was driven by Teo Fabi, the very quick Italian, in 1988, with improving results.

America had always been far and away Porsche's most important export market, and the 962 model had dominated the IMSA Camel Light GTP Championship as well, from 1984 until 1987. After that the going got tougher, with fresh competition from Jaguar and from Nissan.

Indeed the 1988 Le Mans race proved to be the final appearance for a works-entered car, the battlefield being left to the privateers. The last 962C victory in the World Sports-Prototype Championship was at Dijon in 1989. Turbocharged cars would cease to be eligible from 1992. In its ten year life, the 956/962 won 41 races including six Le Mans and five World Championships.

On behalf of the TAG consortium, Porsche designed, developed and prepared the 1.5-litre, turbocharged V6 engines that powered the Marlboro McLaren team, and Niki Lauda and Alain Prost, to three consecutive World Formula 1 Championships between 1984 and 1986. The contract expired at the end of 1987 and then Porsche, in its own right, tackled the specialized world of CART single-seater racing. Hans Mezger and Valentin Schäfer were again responsible for engine design, while the Porsche sports car chassis designer Horst Reitter designed the composite materials monocoque. The car was driven by Teo Fabi, the very quick Italian, in 1988, with improving results and in 1989 at Mid-Ohio Porsche secured its only CART victory with Fabi finishing fourth in the drivers' championship. A year later, at the end of its declared three-year programme Porsche pulled out to concentrate on its new F1 3.5-litre V12 normally aspirated engine in partnership with Footwork Grand Prix International. This was to be a short-lived affair - the under-powered and overweight engine being temporarily withdrawn before mid-season prior to a total pull-out at year end.

Three was certainly unlucky in this context. Chassis no. 001 sidelined four hours into the 1977 Le Mans 24-Hour race.

MARTINI
MARTINI
PORSCHE
DUNLOP
Shell
3
II G TAMPON
STAMP

1978 Le Mans. Car no. 5 was crashed by Jochen Mass after Jacky Ickx had been drafted into the sister car of Barth-Wollék-Joest.

The 936/81 was in fact the old faithful chassis no. 003, rebuilt to the new specification. The engine was a slightly detuned version of the company's stillborn Indy car project. In the hands of Jacky Ickx and Derek Bell, the car led for the whole distance.

Third place in the 1978 Le Mans 24-Hour race went to the 936 driven by Americans Peter Gregg and Hurley Haywood, later with Reinhold Joest.

The stillborn Porsche Indy car project of 1979–80. Having seen the Can-Am championship decimated by the 917, both SCCA and USAC quickly amended their rules to keep out the foreign invader. The rule change simply made it inevitable that Cosworth-engined cars would dominate the series. In essence, the chassis is very similar to the previous year's Parnelli, one of which was used in the engine development stage. The engine was a 2.65-litre flat 6 developed from the 935 and 936, tuned to run on methanol. In 1988 the factory re-entered the battle at Indianapolis. This time resistance on the part of the organizers was lessened by the previous impact of the series-dominating Cosworth engine.

The Indy-developed 2.65-litre engine, with water-cooled cylinder heads and four valves per cylinder, won the 1981 Le Mans with consummate ease, at record speed, and was then used as the basis for the omnipotent 956 Group C car.

A cutaway of the 956 shows Porsche's first monocoque design, and the complications of efficiency-cooling the powerful twin-turbo engine. In many ways the car was the last of a dynasty for the factory; space frames could no longer cope with the FIA crash regulations without some weight penalty.

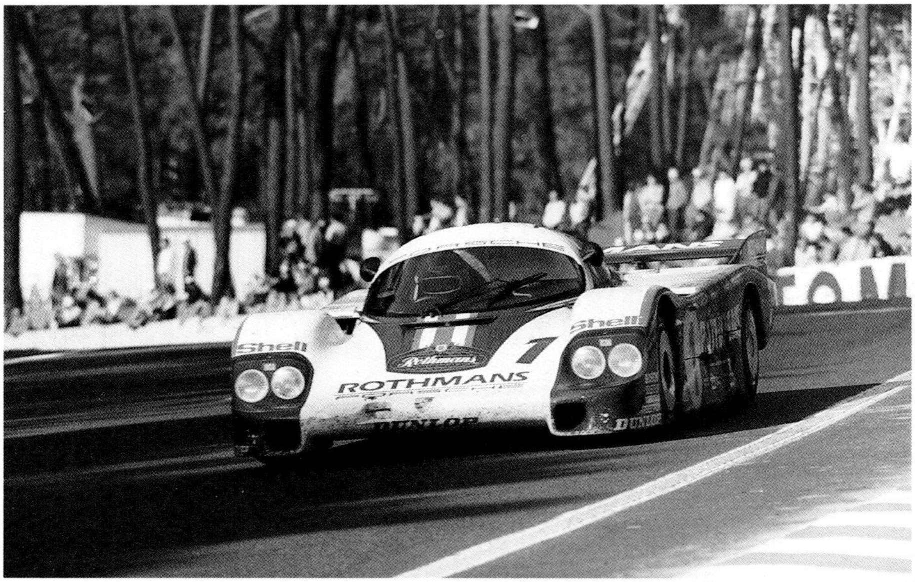

In its Le Mans début the 956 swept all before it, taking the first three positions. This is the Ickx/Bell example on its way to overall honours. For the first time the factory used a monocoque structure, breaking the tradition of space-frames. The body-panels, however, were still fabricated in GRP.

Le Mans 1983. 956-005 racing no. 1, with Ickx and Bell on their way to second overall.

The 1983 Le Mans winner was this 956 driven by the Americans Hurley Haywood and Al Holbert in company with Australian Vern Schuppan. Near the end of the race a door flew off, spoiling the air flow and almost wrecking the engine.

Walter Brun entered two 956s at Spa for the 1984 1000 Kilometres, and the cars finished third and fourth overall. The race was won by the works car of Stefan Bellof and Derek Bell and 956s took the first six places.

Reinhold Joest built his own Group C car based on the type 936 space-frame chassis; the car was the Joest Porsche 936C, campaigned in 1983 for the Belgian Martin brothers under the Belga banner. They failed to finish at Le Mans due to injection problems.

One of the Brun cars at the 1984 Nürburgring 1000 Kilometres. This example driven by Hans Stuck and Harold Grohs, practised second fastest but failed to finish.

Released by the works, Stefan Bellof shared the winning Brun Motorsport car with Hans Stuck at Imola in 1984.

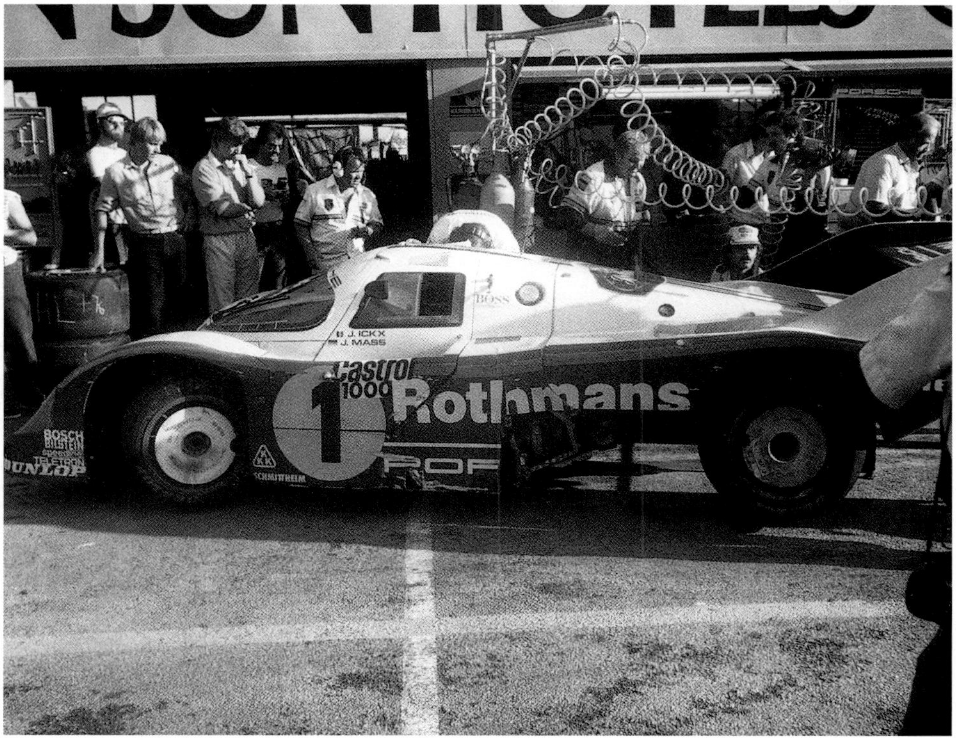

The nightmare of every team manager, as fire breaks out in the works pits at the Hockenheim 1000 Kilometres in 1985. Car no. 1, the Ickx/Mass 956, pressurized the refuelling tower as soon as the hose was connected, and although team manager Norbert Linger was taken to hospital with serious burns both cars continued to race.

The Jacky Ickx/Jochen Mass 956 in the pits at Kyalami, South Africa, in 1983. Despite going off the road when it rained, Ickx's third place was enough for him to retain his World Championship.

The winning car at Le Mans in 1985 was this Joest Racing example handled by Ludwig/Winter/Barilla and sponsored by New Man jeans. The same car had won the race in 1984, driven by Ludwig and Pescarolo.

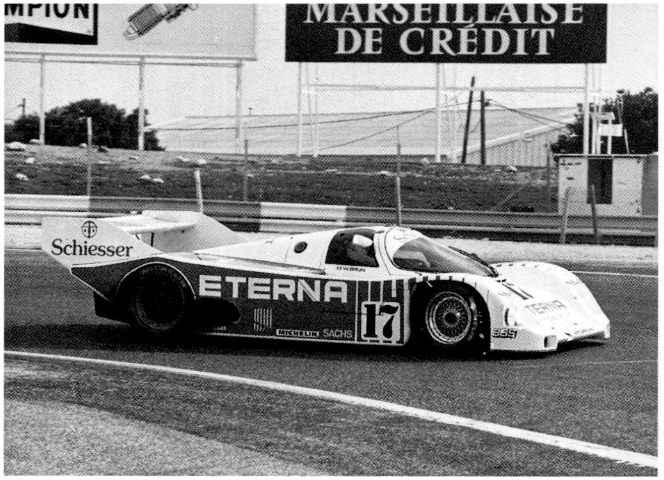

The 962 differed in detail from the 956, many of which were converted to the new specification, due to the uprated safety regulations. The example seen here is the second Brun team car driven by Walter Brun in the Group C ADAC Supercup series in 1986.

The Walter Brun team contested the IMSA series in 1986 with their 962. Here Oscar Larrauri takes the car to second place in the Daytona 24-Hours, with Massimo Sigala and Gianfranco Brancatelli.

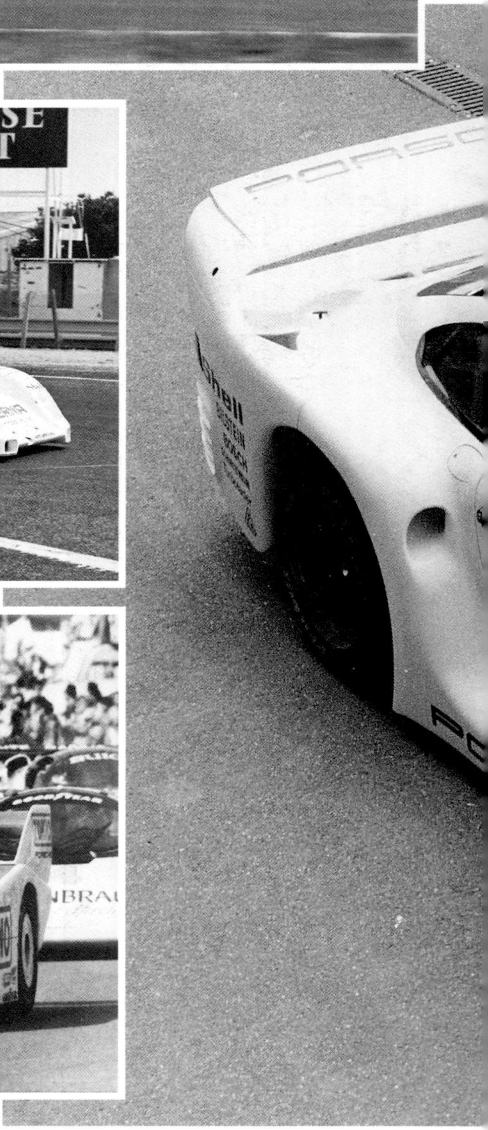

In May 1986 the factory tested the 961 prior to entering the 4-wd cars at Le Mans. As usual, all was satisfactory. The car was in essence the track-going version of the superb 959 roadcar. There were few differences from the roadcars making its seventh place finish even more creditable. It was driven by Paris–Dakar 'Raid' winner René Metge and Claude Ballot-Lena.

8
605233 BG

THE SINGLE-SEAT FORMULA CARS

Rear view of the central seat 550 RSK with which Edgar Barth opened Porsche's Formula 2 account in 1957. Chassis no. 718030, it is now in a private collection in Florida, having passed through the hands of Jean Behra.

Jean Behra at speed in the 1958 Rouen F2 winning car. It was still eligible for GT races, needing only the original nose and some movement of the driving position along with the removal of the special metal tonneau cover.

Dan Gurney on his way to giving Porsche their only Grand Prix victory, at Rouen in 1962. The eight-cylinder engine gave 180bhp at 9200rpm and the car used Porsche's own 718 gearbox with six gears to maximize the narrow torque band. Like all the other monoposto cars, it used torsion bar suspension and, in this instance, disc brakes of Porsche's own design were fitted. The body was in unpainted aluminium over a steel space-frame. Dry weight was 452kg. The car carried the factory series number F1-104.

Jo Bonnier in the purpose-built F2 car waiting for the start at Rheims 1959. Driving for the works, he finished behind the Behra–Porsche. Stirling Moss won in a Cooper Climax.

Jo Bonnier during practice on the Nürburgring in August 1961 with a four-cylinder car, probably 718-2-04. The failure of the injection on the 1961 four-cylinder cars made a return to the older ex-F2 models necessary.

The privately entered Godin de Beaufort car seen from above at the Nürburgring during practice in 1962. At the peak of development these four-cylinder cars were giving up to 190bhp at 8000rpm with Kugelfischer fuel injection.

Giancarlo Baghetti on his way to victory in the 1961 *Coupe Italia* at Vallelunga.

TAG turbo
Techniques d'Avant Garde
PORSCHE

TAG turbo
Techniques d'Avant Garde
PORSCHE

TAG turbo
Techniques d'Avant Garde
PORSCHE

Porsche returned to Formula 1 racing in 1983 with a twin-turbo V6 engine designed, developed and produced for the TAG consortium. It was never, officially, a Porsche engine at all, although Hans Mezger led the Weissach design team. The TAG engine won world championships in 1984, 1985 and 1986, dominating its era. The engine was installed exclusively in McLarens and the champion drivers were Niki Lauda (1984) and Alain Prost (1985 and 1986).

PORSCHE IN THE NINETIES

The year 1990 brought with it a serious blow to Porsche, as to all so-called "Supercar" makers, in the form of a world recession, the depth of which had not been seen for sixty years. It was a very painful experience and caused a massive reduction in sales, especially in the United States of America, where "Porsche" was a name revered in many circles.

Unfortunately, Porsches were the most available of the "Supercar" makes, their price being based on reasoned costs, not charisma. This meant that the "young upwardly mobile" community was better able to afford Porsches - and they were far more reliable than most other "Supercars" anyway. Aston Martins, Ferraris and Lamborghinis were far out of reach of even the most successful young stockbroker, lawyer or dealer whose rise had been heralded with the bubble of the eighties (and which burst in 1989). So they bought Porsches and the effect of that in the recession which followed was that Porsches were associated with that group of people, who used the cars as status symbols, not serious motor cars to be driven with skill and enjoyed for what they were.

This stigma seemed to deal Porsche a cruel blow, one which took a long time from which to recover. Then, barely had the Company begun to crystallise an expansion in sales than the German economy began to flounder in 1993, the consequence of the costs of re-unification. However, in that year, Porsche seemed to be recovering its markets again, with renewing sales in Britain and North America.

The great quality of Porsche is that it has found the key to that "Holy Grail" of the motor industry, the compromise between high design, quality and volume manufacture which has produced a "Supercar" at a realistic price. That may seem a bold statement to make, when you consider a Porsche costs perhaps twice the price of an Audi of similar engine size, until you realise that it costs less than half the price of most of those cars with which it finds itself in competition.

Porsche is a unique phenomenon. After all, how many other cars have had the benefit of being designed by a man with some of the most significant design experience in the industry - the designer of all-conquering Grand Prix cars, the world's first true "People's Car" and the remarkable "Tiger" battle tank? Remember, too, that the first Porsche cars were born directly out of that "People's Car". So that unusual blend of fine design, cost effectiveness in manufacture and mechanical durability are perhaps unmatched.

As we move towards the middle 1990s, the quite remarkable Porsche 911 undoubtedly remains the flagship of the product range. Few cars of any category manage to remain in production for as long as thirty years, as the 911 has done, and even more remarkable is the fact that this one car has remained in production and consistently improved over its whole production life. Yes, it is now a cult, albeit an expensive one as cults go, but the 911 is also a car which leaves an indelible impression on its first-time driver.

Much of the 911's longevity can be credited to the fact that it has no direct rival anywhere in the world, even thirty years after its birth. Certainly, it has improved in handling, in performance and in body life. The early cars, if not cared for lovingly, soon began to decay. They were not the most forgiving in difficult driving situations and even today, the 911 requires a different driving technique from most cars. But the performance, which was sparkling in 1963, has not only kept pace with developments in the industry at large, it has improved to the level of being outstanding, with a near doubling of engine capacity along the way. Which all adds up to a car far ahead of its time when first launched.

The 928 has been around for some years, too, celebrating its fifteenth birthday in 1993 - half the age of the 911. So it, too, has been thoroughly "de-bugged" and of course, has undergone expansion of engine capacity, from 4.5 litres to 5.4 litres in the GTS. It, too, is no slouch and it has the advantage of being a four-seat car, whereas the 911 could never have been truly labelled so.

The 928 does have more identifiable competitors though, than the 911. For example, the Jaguar XJS and more recently, the Aston Martin DB7, instantly come to mind as suitors for the position of the 928 - and the Jaguar has the distinction of being in the same age bracket, though far from equal performance and handling - and not the same charisma. The Aston Martin, on the other hand, may be another story, for this car breaks new ground for the Newport Pagnell-based Ford subsidiary. This is their first steel-bodied car, their first production supercharged car and one aimed head-on at the competition from the Porsche 928. Like the 928, the DB7 is front-engined and a virtual full-four seater. What it might lack in performance against the Porsche, it certainly makes up for in luxury finish. But time alone will tell, for once more, Porsche's experience in volume manufacture - and the price advantage of the 928, will stand in its favour.

The 944 Turbo entered the 1990s in fine form, with a new 3-litre engine which, unbeknown to the world at large, was destined for the car's successor, the 968, which would be announced for 1992.

Still the flagship of the Porsche model range - and the fastest at 171mph - the 928 Series was further developed for the start of 1992. The new 928 GTS features a 5.4-litre version of the familiar 32-valve V8 engine, 17-inch "Cup Design" wheels and lower profile tyres, Turbo style door mirrors, wider rear wheel arches and a reflection strip across the rear, à la 911!

Typically Porsche, the 968 came along as the extensive development of an earlier model, the difference being that the earlier model number was changed - twice - for this car started life as the 924, was extensively developed into the 944 and ultimately gestated into the 968, all with the same basic floorpan, but with an engine which has increased in size by fifty per cent along the way and with styling which has brought it into the 1990s. To use the modern jargon, this is Porsche's "entry-level" model, the first new car of the make likely to be bought by many aspiring Porsche owners.

Whilst the 924 sold in large numbers, it tended to be labelled as the "poor man's" Porsche. This was dispelled to some degree on the arrival of the 944, which was accepted as a real Porsche, though it tended to be regarded as the car an aspiring 928 owner would buy if he couldn't afford a 928. But then came the 968, now established as a true Porsche, whilst unashamedly recognising that it was an "entry level" car, though one with very positive Porsche character.

As the Nineteen Nineties advance, so Porsche has advanced and its three-model line-up, constantly improved as it is, stands it in good stead to face the onset of the Second Millenium with confidence. No other make of car has won Le Mans so many times. No other make of "Supercar" has quite the attainability.

From the rear, the 968 bears more than a strong resemblance to the 928 Series with its uniform red rear light clusters and polyurethane deformable panel concealing the bumper. The model designation is now centrally placed as on the 911 and 928 Series.

Still the most magnificent road Porsche of all is, perhaps, the 911, celebrating its 30th birthday in 1993 and seen here in Carrera 2 Coupé form.

APPENDIX Porsche Models and their Chassis Numbers

Below is a list of Porsche models and their brief specification, beginning with the first 356, built at Gmünd, listed in Type Number sequence. The models are listed in chronological order of production and the year quoted in Column 2 is the first year of build, where more than one year applies. The Chassis Numbers are given in the number blocks as applied to each model type by the manufacturer and other standard specification features follow. Certain small batches of cars (such as sports-competition cars) were built within larger blocks of chassis numbers and so the first and last number of a given group cannot always be taken as the first and last chassis numbers of a particular model - for example, a batch of 25 cars may have been built within a block of chassis numbers a thousand or more apart. Also, some cars were fitted with more than one engine of different capacities. In this case, the original engine size is quoted in this appendix. Every attempt has been made to ensure the accuracy of this data, but the authors apologise if errors have crept into the transcription of the data given here.

MODEL/TYPE	YEAR	CHASSIS NUMBERS	WB-MM	TRACK F/R	BORE/STROKE	CC
356/001 Roadster	1948	001	2150	1290/1250	75 x 64	1131
356/2 (Gmünd) Coupé/Cabriolet	1948	2.001 - 2.050 & 2.052	2100	1290/1250	73.5 x 64	1086
356-Alu (Gmünd) Aluminium Coupe	1949	2.053 - 2.055	2100	1290/1250	73.5 x 64	1086
356 1100 Coupé/Cabriolet/Sports Coupé	1950	5001 - 5600	2100	1290/1250	73.5 x 64	1086
356 1100 Coupé/Sports Coupé	1951	10001 - 10170	2100	1290/1250	73.5 x 64	1086
	1952	11126 - 12084	2100	1290/1250	73.5 x 64	1086
356 1300 Coupé	1952	50001 - 50098	2100	1250/1290	80 x 64	1286
	1953	50099 - 53008	2100	1290/1250	73.5 x 64	1086
540 American Roadster	1951		2100	1290/1250	73.5 x 64	1086
356 1300 Cabriolet	1951	10350 - 10432	2100	1290/1250	80 x 64	1286
356 1500 Cabriolet (	1951	10433 - 10469	2100	1290/1250	80 x 74	1488
(	1951	10531 - 11125	2100	1290/1250	80 x 74	1488
(	1952	12301 - 12387	2100	1290/1250	80 x 74	1488
356 1500S Cabriolet	1952	15001 - 15116	2100	1290/1250	80 x 74	1488
356 1300/1300S Cabriolet	1953	) (	2100	1250/1290	80 x 64	1286
356 1500/1500S Cabriolet	1953	) 60001 - 61000 (	2100	1250/1290	80 x 74	1488
356 1300/1300A/1300S Speedster	1954	80001 - 80200	2100	1250/1290	80 x 64	1286
Type 550-1500RS Sports-racing Spyder	1954	5500001 - 5500090	2100	1290/1250	85 x 66	1498
356A 1500GS de Luxe Coupé	1955	12235 - 12387	2100	1306/1272	85 x 66	1498
	1955	53456 - 59090	2100	1306/1272	85 x 66	1498
	1955	55001 - 55390	2100	1306/1272	85 x 66	1498
356 1300 Coupé	1955	53009 - 55000	2100	1290/1250	74.5 x 74	1290
356 1500/1500S Speedster	1955	80201 - 81900	2100	1290/1250	80 x 74	1488
356A 1300 Coupé/1300S Sports Coupé	1955	55001 - 59090	2100	1306/1272	74.5 x 74	1290
356A 1600S Sports Coupé	1955	55001 - 55390	2100	1306/1272	82.5 x 74	1588
356A 1300S Cabriolet/1300S Sports Cabrio	1955	61001 - 61499	2100	1306/1272	74.5 x 74	1290
356A 1500GS Cabriolet	1955	61001 - 61892	2100	1306/1272	85 x 66	1498
356A 1600S Cabriolet	1955	61001 - 61982	2100	1306/1272	82.5 x 74	1588
356A 1600/1600S Speedster (	1955	81901 - 83691	2100	1306/1272	82.5 x 74	1582
(	1957	83792 - 84922	2100	1306/1272	82.5 x 74	1582
Type 550A-1500RS Sports-racing Spyder	1956	550A0101 - 550A0144	2100	1290/1250	85 x 66	1498
356A 1300S Coupé	1957	100001 - 101692	2100	1306/1272	74.5 x 74	1290
356A 1600 Coupé	1957	101693 - 108917	2100	1306/1272	82.5 x 74	1582
356A 1500GS/1500GS-GT Coupé	1957	58312 - 59090	2100	1306/1272	85 x 66	1498
356A 1600S/1600 Cabriolet	1957	61500 - 61892	2100	1306/1272	82.5 x 74	1582
356A 1600GS/1600GS-GT Speedster	1958	84938 - 85886	2100	1306/1272	87.5 x 66	1588
356A 1600S/1600 Cabriolet	1958	150001 - 152475	2100	1306/1272	82.5 x 74	1582
356A 1600GS/1600GS-GT Cab/356B 1600GS-GT Cpé	1958	104524 - 106174	2100	1306/1272	87.5 x 66	1588
356A 1600S Convertible	1958	85501 - 86830	2100	1306/1272	82.5 x 74	1582
356A 1600GS/1600GS-GT Coupé	1958	150001 - 153334	2100	1306/1272	87.5 x 66	1588
Formula 2 Type 718 Single-seater	1958	718201 - 718204	2200	1300/1260	85 x 66	1498
Type 718-1500RSK Sports-racing Spyder	1958	718001 - 718034	2100	1290/1250	85 x 66	1498
Type 718 RS 60/718 RS 61 Spyder	1959	718051 - 718078	2100	1290/1250	85 x 66	1498
356B 1600 Coupé	1959	108916 - 117476	2100	1306/1272	82.5 x 74	1582
	1961	118951 - 125239	2100	1306/1272	82.5 x 74	1582
Type 718 RS 61 Coupé Le Mans/718 (62) Spyder	1961	718044 - 718047	2335	1300/1280	76 x 54.6	1982
356B 1600S Coupé	1961	117601 - 118950	2100	1306/1272	82.5 x 74	1582
356B 2000GS Coupé	1961	119289 - 121099	2100	1306/1272	92 x 74	1966

MODEL/TYPE	YEAR	CHASSIS NUMBERS			WB-MM	TRACK F/R	BORE/STROKE	CC
356B 1600S Cabriolet	1959	152476	-	155569	2100	1306/1272	82.5 x 74	1582
356B 1600/1600-90/1600S-90 Cabriolet	1961	155601	-	158700	2100	1306/1272	82.5 x 74	1582
356B 1600S/1600S-90 Roadster	1959	86831	-	89483	2100	1306/1272	82.5 x 74	1582
	1961	89601	-	89849	2100	1306/1272	82.5 x 74	1582
Formula 2 Type 718/787 Single seater	1960			718205	2200	1300/1260	85 x 66	1498
Monoposto Formula 2 Type 787	1960	78701	-	78702	2300	1300/1290	85 x 66	1498
356B 1600GTL Abarth Coupé	1960	11011	-	11021	2100	1306/1272	87.5 x 66	1588
356B 1600S-90 K-Hardtop	1961	200001	-	201048	2100	1306/1272	82.5 x 74	1582
356B 1600S/1600-90 K-Hardtop	1961	201601	-	202299	2100	1306/1272	82.5 x 74	1582
Formula 1 Grand Prix Type 804	1961	80401	-	80404	2300	1300/1330	66 x 54.6	1494
356B 1600S/1600-90 K-Hardtop	1961	201601	-	202299	2100	1306/1272	82.5 x 74	1582
356B 1600S-90 K-Coupé	1962	210001	-	214400	2100	1306/1272	82.5 x 74	1582
356C 1600C Coupé	1963	126001	-	131930	2100	1306/1272	82.5 x 74	1582
356C 1600C K-Coupé	1963	215001	-	222579	2100	1306/1272	82.5 x 74	1582
356C 1600SC Cabriolet	1963	159001	-	162165	2100	1306/1272	82.5 x 74	1582
356C 2000GS Coupé	1963	119289	-	125239	2100	1306/1272	92 x 74	1966
	1963	156566	-	158700	2100	1306/1272	92 x 74	1966
901 2.0 Coupé	1963	------			2204	1332/1312	80 x 66	1991
911 2.0 Coupé	1963	300001	-	305100	2211	1337/1317	80 x 66	1991
904-6/904-8 Competition Coupé	1964	904001	-	904006	2300	1314/1312	92 x 74	1966
904GTS Competition Coupé	1964	904007	-	904106	2300	1316/1312	80 x 54.6	2195
Elva-Porsche Competition Spyder	1964	No chassis number			2286	1270/1350	80 x 54.6	2195
906-8 Competition Spyder	1965	906007	-	906009	2300	1338/1402	76 x 54.6	1981
906-8 Spyder "Lotus" (Lotus running gear)	1965			906010	2300	1340/1410	76 x 54.6	1981
911 2.0 Coupé "Monte"	1965	303075-076	&	303085	2211	1367/1339	80 x 66	1991
	1965	305101	-	308522	2211	1353/1325	80 x 66	1991
912 1600 Coupé	1965	350001	-	351970	2211	1337/1317	82.5 x 74	1582
912 1600 K-Coupé	1965	450001	-	461140	2211	1337/1317	82.5 x 74	1582
906-6 Competition Coupé	1966	906101	-	906158	2300	1338/1402	80 x 66	1991
906-6 Competition Coupé LH	1966	906001	-	906003	2300	1338/1402	80 x 66	1991
910-6/910-8/910-6-LH Competition Coupé	1966	910001	-	910028	2300	1430/1401	80 x 66	1991
910-8 Competition Spyder	1966	910030	-	910034	2300	1430/1401	76 x 54.6	1981
912 1600 Coupé	1966	351971	-	354000	2211	1337/1317	82.5 x 74	1582
	1966	354001	-	354970	2211	1353/1321	82.5 x 74	1582
912 1600 K-Coupé	1966	454470	-	458100	2211	1337/1317	82.5 x 74	1582
	1966	458101	-	461140	2211	1353/1321	82.5 x 74	1582
911S 2.0 Coupé	1966	305101S	-	308523S	2211	1367/1339	80 x 66	1991
911S 2.0 Targa	1966	500001S	-	500718S	2211	1353/1325	80 x 66	1991
907-8 Competition Coupé	1967	907001-4 + 11 + 022-032			2300	1462/1403	80 x 54.6	2195
907-6 Competition Coupé	1967	907005	-	907008	2300	1462/1403	80 x 66	1991
911S 2.0 Coupé "Rallye"	1967	306655S	-	306657S	2211	1367/1339	80 x 66	1991
911L-US 2.0 Coupé	1967	11805001	-	11805449	2211	1353/1325	80 x 66	1991
911L-US 2.0 Targa	1967	11855001	-	11855134	2211	1353/1325	80 x 66	1991
911L 2.0 Coupé	1967	11800001	-	11810720	2211	1353/1325	80 x 66	1991
911L 2.0 Targa	1967	11860001	-	11860307	2211	1353/1325	80 x 66	1991
911 2.0 Targa	1967	11880001	-	11880268	2211	1353/1325	80 x 66	1991
911 2.0 K-Coupé	1967	11835001	-	11835742	2211	1353/1325	80 x 66	1991
911T 2.0 Coupé	1967	11820001	-	11820928	2211	1353/1325	80 x 66	1991
911T 2.0 K-Coupé	1967	11825001	-	11825683	2211	1353/1325	80 x 66	1991
911T 2.0 Targa	1967	11870001	-	11870521	2211	1353/1325	80 x 66	1991
911S 2.0 Coupé	1967	11800001	-	11801267	2211	1367/1335	80 x 66	1991
911S 2.0 K-Coupé	1967	11800001	-	11801267	2211	1367/1335	80 x 66	1991
911S 2.0 Targa	1967	11850001	-	11850442	2211	1367/1339	80 x 66	1991
911R 2.0 Competition Coupé	1967	305876	&	30670-671	2211	1370/1370	80 x 66	1991
		11899001R	-	11899019R	2211	1370/1370	80 x 66	1991
912 1600 K-Coupé	1967	461141	-	463204	2211	1337/1317	82.5 x 74	1582
912 1600 Coupé	1967	354971	-	355601	2211	1337/1317	82.5 x 74	1582
912 1600 Targa	1967	550001	-	550544	2211	1337/1317	82.5 x 74	1582

MODEL/TYPE	YEAR	CHASSIS NUMBERS	WB-MM	TRACK F/R	BORE/STROKE	CC
909-8 Competition Spyder	1968	909001 - 909002	2264	1470/1464	76 x 54.6	1981
908.01 Competition Coupé	1968	908001 - 908012	2300	1484/1456	85 x 66	2997
908.01 Competition Coupé-LH	1968	908000/02-4/13-16/22-26/29-31	2300	1462/1454	85 x 66	2997
912 1600 K-Coupé	1968	12800001 - 12805598	2211	1337/1317	82.5 x 74	1582
	1968	129020001 - 129023450	2211	1337/1317	82.5 x 74	1582
912 1600 Coupé	1968	12820001 - 12820427	2211	1337/1317	82.5 x 74	1582
	1968	12900001 - 12900428	2211	1337/1317	82.5 x 74	1582
912 1600 Targa	1968	12870001 - 12871217	2211	1337/1317	82.5 x 74	1582
	1968	129010001 - 129010801	2211	1337/1317	82.5 x 74	1582
911T 2.0 Coupé	1968	11900001 - 11900343	2268	1367/1335	80 x 66	1991
911T 2.0 K-Coupé	1968	119120001 - 119123561	2268	1364/1345	80 x 66	1991
911E 2.0 Coupé	1968	119200001 - 119200954	2268	1374/1355	80 x 66	1991
911E 2.0 K-Coupé	1968	119220001 - 119221014	2268	1374/1355	80 x 66	1991
911E 2.0 Targa	1968	119210001 - 119210858	2268	1364/1345	80 x 66	1991
911S 2.0 Coupé	1968	119300001 - 119301492	2268	1367/1335	80 x 66	1991
911S 2.0 Targa	1968	119310001 - 119310614	2268	1374/1355	80 x 66	1991
908.02/908.02-LH Competition Spyder	1969	90802002 - 019/024-8	2300	1486/1454	85 x 66	2997
911T 2.2 Coupé (Manual & Sportomatic)	1969	9110100001 - 9110102418	2268	1362/1343	84 x 66	2195
911T 2.2 K-Coupé (Manual & S/matic)	1969	9110120001 - 9110124126	2268	1362/1343	84 x 66	2195
911T 2.2 Targa (Manual & S/matic)	1969	9110110001 - 9110112545	2268	1362/1343	84 x 66	2195
911E 2.2 Coupé (Manual & S/matic)	1969	9110200001 - 9110201304	2268	1374/1355	84 x 66	2195
911E 2.2 K-Coupé (Manual & S/matic)	1969	9110220001 - 9110220667	2268	1374/1355	84 x 66	2195
911E 2.2 Targa (Manual & S/matic)	1969	9110210001 - 9110210933	2268	1374/1355	84 x 66	2195
911S 2.2 Coupé	1969	9110300001 - 9110301744	2268	1367/1335	80 x 66	1991
917-4.5 Competition Coupé	1969	917001 - 917025	2300	1526/1533	85 x 66	4494
917-PA Competition Spyder	1969	917027	2300	1526/1533	85 x 66	4494
914.4 1.7 Coupé	1969	4702900001 - 4702913312	2450	1337/1374	90 x 66	1679
914.6 2.0 Coupé	1969	9140430001 - 9140432668	2450	1361/1382	80 x 66	1991
916 2.4 Coupé	1969	9142330010 - 9142330020	2450	1386/1480	84 x 70.4	2341
908.03 Competition Spyder	1970	90803001 - 90803013	2300	1504/1510	85 x 66	2997
911S 2.2 Coupé & Coupé "Rallye"	1970	9110300001 - 9110300950	2268	1374/1355	84 x 66	2331
917K 4.5 Competition Coupé/Spyder	1970	) (	2300	1564/1584	85 x 66	4494
917K 4.9 Competition Coupé/Spyder	1970	) (	2300	1564/1584	86 x 70.4	4907
917K 5.0 Competition Coupé/Spyder	1970	) (	2300	1526/1533	86.8x 70.4	4999
917K 5.4 Competition Coupé/Spyder	1970	) 917001 - 917053(	2300	1564/1584	90 x 70.4	5374
917K 4.9 Competition Coupé-LH	1970	917042 - 917043	2300	1564/1584	86 x 70.4	4907
911S 2.3 Coupé	1970	9110300001 - 9110300003	2268	1374/1355	85 x 66	2247
911S 2.4 Coupé Prototype	1970	911030949	2268	1402/1421	85 x 70.4	2395
914.4 1.7 Coupé	1970	4712900001 - 4712916231	2450	1337/1374	90 x 66	1679
914.6 2.0 Coupé	1970	6410011 - 6410268	2450	1361/1382	80 x 66	1991
911T 2.2 Coupé (Manual & S/matic)	1970	9111100001 - 9111100583	2268	1362/1343	84 x 66	2195
911T 2.2 K-Coupé (Manual & S/matic)	1970	9111120001 - 9111121934	2268	1362/1343	84 x 66	2195
911T 2.2 Targa (Manual & S/matic)	1970	9111110001 - 9111113476	2268	1362/1343	84 x 66	2195
911E 2.2 Coupé (Manual & S/matic)	1970	9111200001 - 9111201088	2268	1374/1355	84 x 66	2195
911E 2.2 Targa (Manual & S/matic)	1970	9111210001 - 9111210935	2268	1374/1355	84 x 66	2195
911S 2.2 Coupé	1970	9111300001 - 9111301430	2268	1367/1335	80 x 66	1991
911S 2.2 Targa	1970	9111310001 - 9111310788	2268	1374/1355	84 x 66	2195
914.6 2.0 Coupé	1971	9141430139 - 9141430141	2450	1343/1383	90 x 66	1679
911S 2.2 Coupé "Safari"	1971	9111300561/589/612/637/683	2271	1402/1421	84 x 66	2195
917LH-4.9 Competition Coupé-LH	1971	917026 - 917045	2300	1564/1584	86 x 70.4	4907
917-20-4.9 Competition Coupé	1971	91720001	2300	1564/1584	86 x 70.4	4907
914.4 1.7 Coupé	1971	4722900140 - 4722921580	2450	1337/1374	90 x 66	1679
914.6 2.0 Coupé	1971	9142430001 - 9142430240	2450	1361/1382	80 x 66	1991
911T 2.4 Coupé (Manual & S/matic)	1971	9112500001 - 9112501963	2271	1360/1342	84 x 70.4	2341
911T 2.4 Targa (Manual & S/matic)	1971	9112510001 - 9112511523	2271	1372/1354	84 x 70.4	2341
911T-US 2.4 Coupé (Manual & S/matic)	1971	9112100001 - 9112102931	2271	1360/1342	84 x 70.4	2341
911T-US 2.4 Targa (Manual & S/matic)	1971	9112110001 - 9112111821	2271	1360/1342	84 x 70.4	2341
911E 2.4 Coupé (Manual & S/matic)	1971	9112200001 - 9112201124	2271	1372/1354	84 x 70.4	2341

MODEL/TYPE	YEAR	CHASSIS NUMBERS	WB-MM	TRACK F/R	BORE/STROKE	CC
911E 2.4 Targa (Manual & S/matic)	1971	9112210001 - 9112210861	2271	1372/1354	84 x 70.4	2341
911S 2.4 Coupé (Manual & S/matic)	1971	9112300001 - 9112301750	2271	1372/1354	80 x 70.4	2341
911S 2.4 Targa (Manual & S/matic)	1971	9112310001 - 9112310989	2271	1372/1354	84 x 70.4	2341
911S 2.5 Coupé	1972	9112300041 - 9112300047	2271	1402/1421	89 x 66	2466
917-10-TC-4.5 Competition Spyder	1972	) (	2316	1620/1638	85 x 66	4494
917-10-TC-4.9 Competition Spyder	1972	) (	2500	1620/1638	86.8x 70.4	4999
917-10-TC-5.4 Competition Spyder	1972	) (	2500	1620/1638	90 x 70.4	5374
917-10-6.5 Competition Spyder	1972	) 91710001 - 91710018(	2500	1620/1638	86 x 70.4	6543
911T 2.4 Coupé (Manual & S/matic)	1972	9113500001 - 9113501875	2271	1360/1342	84 x 70.4	2341
911T 2.4 Targa (Manual & S/matic)	1972	9113510001 - 9113511541	2271	1360/1342	84 x 70.4	2341
911T-US 2.4 Coupé (Manual & S/matic)	1972	9113100001 - 9113101252	2271	1360/1342	84 x 70.4	2341
911T-US 2.4 Targa (Manual & S/matic)	1972	9113110001 - 9113110781	2271	1360/1342	84 x 70.4	2341
911T-C 2.4 Coupé (Manual & S/matic)	1972	9113101501 - 9113103444	2271	1360/1342	84 x 70.4	2341
911T-C 2.4 Targa (Manual & S/matic)	1972	9113110001 - 9113112303	2271	1372/1354	84 x 70.4	2341
911E 2.4 Coupé (Manual & S/matic)	1972	9113200001 - 9113201366	2271	1372/1354	84 x 70.4	2341
911E 2.4 Targa (Manual & S/matic)	1972	9113210001 - 9113211055	2271	1372/1354	84 x 70.4	2341
911S 2.4 Coupé (Manual & S/matic)	1972	9113300001 - 9113301430	2271	1372/1354	80 x 70.4	2341
911S 2.4 Targa (Manual & S/matic)	1972	9113310001 - 9113310925	2271	1372/1354	84 x 70.4	2341
911SC 2.4 Coupé	1972	9113600001 - 9113601590	2271	1372/1394	80 x 70.4	2341
914.4 1.7 Coupé	1972	4732900001 - 4732927660	2450	1343/1383	90 x 66	1679
917-30-TC Competition Spyder	1973	91730002 - 91730003	2500	1670/1564	90 x 70.4	5374
914.4 1.7 Coupé	1973	4742900001 - onwards	2450	1343/1383	90 x 66	1679
911RS 2.7 Carrera RS ("F" Series) Coupé	1973	9113600001 - 9113601036	2271	1372/1372	90 x 70.4	2687
911SC 2.7 Coupé	1973	9113601590 - onwards	2271	1394/1394	90 x 70.4	2687
911SC Carrera 2.7 "Safari"	1973	9113600285 - 9113600288	2271	1372/1394	90 x 70.4	2687
911SC Carrera 2.8 RSR	1973	9113600386 - 9113600685?	2271	1402/1421	92 x 70.4	2806
911SC Carrera RSR "Proto"	1973	911360019/20/307/328/526/			90 x 70.4	2687
		588/686/974	2271	1472/1578	95 x 70.4	2993
911RSR-TC Carrera Turbo	1974	9113600576/4609016/9101-2	2271	1472/1578	83 x 66	2142
911 2.7 Coupé (Manual & S/matic)	1974	9114100001 - 9114104041	2271	1360/1342	90 x 70.4	2687
911 2.7 Targa (Manual & S/matic)	1974	9114110001 - 9114113110	2271	1372/1354	90 x 70.4	2687
911S 2.7 Coupé (Manual & S/matic)	1974	9114300001 - 9114301359	2271	1360/1342	90 x 70.4	2687
911S 2.7 Targa (Manual & S/matic)	1974	9114310001 - 9114310898	2271	1372/1354	90 x 70.4	2687
911SC 2.7-US Carrera ("G") Coupé-US	1974	9114400001 - 9114400528	2271	1360/1342	90 x 70.4	2687
911 2.7-US Targa (Manual & S/matic)	1974	9114410001 - 9114410246	2271	1372/1380	90 x 70.4	2687
911SC 2.7 Carrera ("G" Series) Coupé	1974	9114600001 - 9114601036	2271	1372/1354	90 x 70.4	2687
911SC 2.7 Carrera ("G" Series) Targa	1974	9114610001 - 9114610433	2271	1372/1380	90 x 70.4	2687
911RS 3.0 Carrera RS Coupé	1974	9114609001 - 9114609109	2271	1437/1462	95 x 70.4	2993
911RSR 3.0 Carrera RSR Coupé	1974	9114619001 - 9114619109	2271	1360/1342	90 x 70.4	2687
908.03-Turbo Competition Spyder	1975	90803008 - 90803011	2300	1542/1506	83 x 66	2142
912E 2.0 Coupé	1975	9126000001 - 9126002099	2271	1360/1330	94 x 71.1	1971
911 2.7 Coupé (Manual & S/matic)	1975	9115100001 - 9115101238	2271	1372/1354	90 x 70.4	2687
911 2.7 Targa (Manual & S/matic)	1975	9115110001 - 9115110998	2271	1372/1380	90 x 70.4	2687
911S-US 2.7 Coupé (Manual & S/matic)	1975	9115200001 - 9115202310	2271	1372/1342	90 x 70.4	2687
911S-US 2.7 Targa (Manual & S/matic)	1975	9115210001 - 9115211517	2271	1372/1368	90 x 70.4	2687
911S 2.7 Coupé (Manual & S/matic)	1975	9115300001 - 9115300385	2271	1372/1354	90 x 70.4	2687
911S 2.7 Targa (Manual & S/matic)	1975	9115310001 - 9115310266	2271	1372/1380	90 x 70.4	2687
911SC 2.7 Carrera-US Coupé (Manual-S/matic)	1975	9115400001 - 9115400395	2271	1372/1342	90 x 70.4	2687
911SC 2.7 Carrera-US Targa (Manual-S/matic)	1975	9115410001 - 9115410174	2271	1372/1368	90 x 70.4	2687
911SC 2.7 Carrera Coupé ("H" Series)	1975	9115600001 - 9115600518	2271	1372/1354	90 x 70.4	2687
911SC 2.7 Carrera Targa ("H" Series)	1975	9115610001 - 9115610197	2271	1372/1380	90 x 70.4	2687
911 3.0 Coupé (Manual & S/matic)	1975	9116600001 - 9116601093	2271	1372/1380	95 x 70.4	2993
911 3.0 Targa (Manual & S/matic)	1975	9116610001 - 9116610479	2271	1372/1380	95 x 70.4	2993
930 Turbo 3.0 Coupé (Manual & S/matic)	1975	9305700001 - 9305700284	2271	1432/1501	95 x 70.4	2993
934 Turbo Competition Coupé	1976	9306700151 - 9306700180/540	2269	1481/1496	95 x 70.4	2993
935-TC Turbo Coupé Group 5 Prototype	1976	9305700002-R15	2271	1502/1558	92 x 70.4	2806
936-TC Turbo Spyder Group 6	1976	936001 - 936002	2400	1580/1510	83 x 66	2142
935 Competition Coupé	1976	9305700002-R15 (updated)	2271	1502/1558	92 x 70.4	2857

MODEL/TYPE	YEAR	CHASSIS NUMBERS	WB-MM	TRACK F/R	BORE/STROKE	CC
935 Turbo Competition Coupé	1976	935001 - 935002	2271	1502/1558	92 x 70.4	2857
911 2.7 Coupé (Japan)	1976	9116100001 - 9116100130	2271	1372/1354	90 x 70.4	2687
911S-US 2.7 Coupé (Manual & S/matic)	1976	9116200001 - 9116202079	2271	1372/1342	90 x 70.4	2687
911S-US 2.7 Targa (Manual & S/matic)	1976	9116210001 - 9116212175	2271	1372/1342	90 x 70.4	2687
911 2.7 Coupé (Manual & S/matic)	1976	9116300001 - 9116301868	2271	1372/1354	90 x 70.4	2687
911 2.7 Targa (Manual & S/matic)	1976	9116310001 - 9116311576	2271	1372/1380	90 x 70.4	2687
911 2.7 Coupé 210 bhp	1976	9116609001 - 9116609123	2271	1360/1342	90 x 70.4	2687
911 2.7 Targa 210 bhp	1976	9116619001 - 9116619030	2271	1360/1342	90 x 70.4	2687
930 Turbo 3.0 Coupé	1976	9306700001 - 9306700644	2271	1432/1501	95 x 70.4	2993
930 Turbo-US 3.0 Coupé	1976	9306800001 - 9306800530	2271	1432/1501	95 x 70.4	2993
924 2.0 Coupé	1976	9246100001 - 9246105145	2400	1418/1372	86.5x 84.4	1984
935 Turbo 3.0 Coupé	1977	9307700901 - 9307700913	2271	1502/1588	92.8x 70.4	2857
934-US Turbo 3.0 Coupé-US	1977	9307700951 - 9307700960	2271	1481/1496	95 x 70.4	2993
935-77 Turbo 2.8 Competition Coupé	1977	935.77003 - 935.77005	2271	1502/1558	92.8x 70.4	2857
935-77-20 Turbo 1.4 Competition Coupé	1977	935.2.001	2271	1502/1457	71 x 60	1425
936-77 Turbo 2.1 Competition Spyder	1977	936001 - 936002	2410	1530/1480	83 x 66	2142
911 2.7 Coupé (Manual & S/matic)	1977	9117300001 - 9117302449	2271	1369/1354	90 x 70.4	2687
911 2.7 Targa (Manual & S/matic)	1977	9117310001 - 9117311724	2271	1369/1354	90 x 70.4	2687
911S-US 2.7 Coupé (Manual & S/matic)	1977	9117200001 - 9117203388	2271	1369/1354	90 x 70.4	2687
911T-US 2.4 Targa (Manual & S/matic)	1977	9117210001 - 9117212747	2271	1369/1354	90 x 70.4	2687
911 2.7 Coupé (Japan - Manual & S/matic)	1977	911	2271	1369/1354	90 x 70.4	2687
911 2.7 Targa (Japan - Manual & S/matic)	1977	911	2271	1369/1354	90 x 70.4	2687
911 3.0 Coupé (Manual & S/matic)	1977	9117600001 - 9117601473	2271	1372/1380	95 x 70.4	2993
911 3.0 Targa (Manual & S/matic)	1977	9117610001 - 9117610646	2271	1372/1380	95 x 70.4	2993
930 Turbo 3.0 Coupé	1977	9307700001 - 9307700695	2272	1438/1511	95 x 70.4	2993
930-US Turbo 3.0 Coupé-US	1977	9307800001 - 9307800727	2272	1438/1511	95 x 70.4	2993
924 2.0 Coupé Automatic	1977	9247100001 - 9247108512	2400	1418/1372	86.5x 84.4	1984
924 2.0 Coupé-US Automatic	1977	9247230001 - 9247235789	2400	1418/1372	86.5x 84.4	1984
924 2.0 Coupé-US	1977	9247200001 - 9247209163	2400	1418/1372	86.5x 84.4	1984
924 2.0 Coupé - Japan	1977	9247300001 - 9247300261	2400	1418/1372	86.5x 84.4	1984
924 2.0 Coupé Automatic - Japan	1977	9247330001 - 9247330164	2400	1418/1372	86.5x 84.4	1984
924 2.0 Coupé-US Automatic	1977	9247210001 - 9247211767	2400	1418/1372	86.5x 84.4	1984
935-78 Turbo 2.8 Competition Coupé	1978	935.78006 - 935.78007	2271	1502/1588	92.8x 70.4	2857
935-78 Turbo Competition Coupé ("Customer")	1978	9308900011 - 9308900033	2271	1502/1558	92.8x 70.4	2857
935-78 Turbo Competition Coupé (Works)	1978	935006 - 935007	2279	1630/1575	95.7x 74.4	3211
936-78 Turbo 2.1 Competition Spyder	1978	936003 (rebuilt)	2430	1530/1480	87 x 60	2140
924 Rally 2.0 Coupé	1978	9247100013 + 15 + 16 + 19	2400	1418/1392	86.5x 84.4	1984
911SC-US 3.0 Coupé-US (Manual-S/matic)	1978	9118200001 - 9118202436	2272	1361/1367	95 x 70.4	2993
911-US 3.0 California Targa (Manual-S/matic)	1978	9118210001 - 9118212597	2272	1361/1367	95 x 70.4	2993
911SC 3.0 Coupé (Manual & S/matic)	1978	9118300001 - 9118302438	2272	1369/1379	95 x 70.4	2993
911 3.0 Coupé-Japan	1978	9118309501 - 9118309804	2271	1361/1367	95 x 70.4	2993
911SC 3.0 Targa (Manual & S/matic)	1978	9118310001 - 9118311729	2272	1369/1379	95 x 70.4	2993
930 Turbo 3.3 Coupé	1978	9308700001 - 9308700735	2272	1432/1501	97 x 74.4	3299
930-US Turbo 3.3 Coupé-US	1978	9308800001 - 9308800461	2272	1432/1501	97 x 74.4	3299
930 Turbo 3.3 Coupé-Japan	1978	9308709501 - 9308709561	2272	1432/1501	97 x 74.4	3299
924 2.0 Coupé (incl Automatic)	1978	9248100001 - 9248109474	2400	1418/1372	86.5x 84.4	1984
924 2.0 Coupé-US	1978	9248200001 - 9248211638	2400	1418/1372	86.5x 84.4	1984
924 2.0 Coupé - Japan	1978	9248330001 - 9248330450	2400	1418/1372	86.5x 84.4	1984
928 4.5 Coupé (Manual & Automatic)	1978	9288100001 - 9288102646	2500	1551/1530	95 x 78.9	4474
928 4.5 Coupé - Japan	1978	9288209501 - 9288209575	2500	1551/1530	95 x 78.9	4474
928-USA 4.5 Coupé - US (Automatic)	1978	9288200001 - 9288201139	2500	1551/1530	95 x 78.9	4474
935-79 Turbo Competition Coupé	1979	00000009 - 00000013	2271	1502/1558	97 x 70.4	3124
935-79 Turbo Competition Coupé ("Customer")	1979	00016-17 + 00022-25 + 27-28	2271	1502/1558	95 x 74.4	3160
911SC-US 3.0 Coupé - US	1979	9119200001 - 9119202013	2272	1369/1367	95 x 70.4	2993
911SC-US 3.0 California Targa	1979	9119210001 - 9119211965	2272	1369/1379	95 x 70.4	2993
911SC 3.0 Coupé	1979	9119300001 - 9119303319	2272	1369/1379	95 x 70.4	2993
911SC 3.0 Coupé - Japan	1979	9119309501 - 9119309873	2272	1369/1379	95 x 70.4	2993
911SC 3.0 Targa	1979	9119310001 - 9119313319	2272	1369/1379	95 x 70.4	2993

MODEL/TYPE	YEAR	CHASSIS NUMBERS	WB-MM	TRACK F/R	BORE/STROKE	CC
924 Rally 2.0 Coupé	1979	93A0190001	2400	1477/1476	86.5x 84.4	1984
924 2.0 Competition Coupé SCCA	1979	92A0490001 - 94A0490016	2400	1513/1466	87.7x 84.4	2039
Indy P6B Monoposto	1979	P6BF-051P1	2430	1530/1480	92.3 x 66	2650
924 2.0 Coupé (Automatic RHD)	1979	9249100001 - 9249100475	2400	1418/1372	86.5x 84.4	1984
924 2.0 Coupé-US California (Automatic)	1979	9249200001 - 9249209636	2400	1418/1372	86.5x 84.4	1984
924 2.0 Coupé-Japan (Automatic)	1979	9249330001 - 9249330508	2400	1418/1372	86.5x 84.4	1984
924 2.0 Turbo Coupé	1979	9249400001 - 9249401982	2400	1418/1392	86.5x 84.4	1984
924 2.0 Turbo Coupé - USA	1979	9249500001 - 9249504950	2400	1418/1392	86.5x 84.4	1984
928 4.5 Coupé (Manual/Automatic)	1979	9289100001 - 9289103059	2500	1551/1530	95 x 78.9	4474
928-USA 4.5 Coupé - USA (Manual/Automatic)	1979	9289200001 - 9289202285	2500	1551/1530	95 x 78.9	4474
928 4.5 Coupé - Japan (Manual/Automatic)	1979	9289209501 - 9289209623	2500	1551/1530	95 x 78.9	4474
911SC 3.0 Coupé/Targa	1980	91A0130001 - 91A0134831	2272	1369/1379	95 x 70.4	2993
911SC-US 3.0 Coupé/Targa - USA	1980	91A0140001 - 91A0144272	2272	1369/1379	95 x 70.4	2993
924 2.0 Coupé Le Mans GTP	1980	924 001 - 924 004	2400	1534/1504	86.5x 84.4	1984
924 2.0 Coupé (RHD)	1980	92A0410001 - 92A0419094	2400	1418/1372	86.5x 84.4	1984
924 Automatic Coupé - USA	1980	92A0430001 - 92A0433700	2400	1418/1372	86.5x 84.4	1984
924 Automatic Coupé - Japan	1980	92A0440001 - 92A04?	2400	1418/1372	86.5x 84.4	1984
924 2.0 Turbo Coupé	1980	93A0140001 - 93A0141803	2400	1418/1392	86.5x 84.4	1984
924 2.0 Turbo Coupé - USA	1980	93A0150001 - 93A0153440	2400	1418/1372	86.5x 84.4	1984
924 2.0 Coupé Carrera GT	1980	93BN700001-00006 - 00450	2400	1418/1372	86.5x 84.4	1984
928 4.5 Coupé (Manual/Auto - incl Japan)	1980	92A0800001 - 92A0801192	2500	1552/1529	95 x 78.9	4474
928-USA 4.5 Coupé - USA (Manual/Automatic)	1980	92A0810001 - 92A0801649	2500	1552/1529	95 x 78.9	4474
936-81 Turbo Competition Spyder	1981	rebuilt 936001 and 936003	2430	1530/1480	92.3 x 66	2650
924 2.0 Coupé Carrera GTR Turbo	1981	WPOZZZ93--BS72001 - 93BS72025	2400	1534/1504	86.5x 84.4	1984
911SC 3.0 Coupé	1981	WPOZZZ91ZBS100001 -	2272	1369/1379	95 x 70.4	2993
911 3.0 Targa	1981	WPOZZZ91ZBS140001 -	2272	1372/1380	95 x 70.4	2993
911-US 3.0 Coupé - USA	1981	WPOAA091-BS120001 -	2272	1369/1379	95 x 70.4	2993
911-US 3.0 Targa - USA	1981	WPOAA091-BS160001 -	2272	1372/1380	95 x 70.4	2993
930 3.3 Turbo Coupé	1981	WPOZZZ93ZBS000001 -	2272	1369/1379	97 x 74.4	3299
911 3.3 Turbo Coupé - Canada	1981	WPOJA093-BS050001 -	2272	1369/1379	97 x 74.4	3299
924 2.0 Coupé (RHD)	1981		2400	1418/1372	86.5x 84.4	1984
924 2.0 Coupé Automatic	1981		2400	1418/1372	86.5x 84.4	1984
924-US 2.0 Coupé - USA	1981		2400	1418/1372	86.5x 84.4	1984
924-US 2.0 California Automatic Coupé	1981		2400	1418/1372	86.5x 84.4	1984
924 2.0 Coupé - Japan	1981		2400	1418/1372	86.5x 84.4	1984
924 2.0 Coupé Turbo	1981		2400	1418/1372	86.5x 84.4	1984
924-US 2.0 Coupé Turbo - USA	1981		2400	1418/1372	86.5x 84.4	1984
924 2.0 Coupé Turbo - Japan	1981		2400	1418/1372	86.5x 84.4	1984
924 2.0 Coupé Carrera GTS Turbo	1981	WPOZZZ92-BN471001 - BN471050	2400	1418/1372	86.5x 84.4	1984
928 4.5 Coupé (Manual/Automatic)	1981	WPOZZZ92ZBS800001 -	2500	1552/1529	95 x 78.9	4474
928-US 4.5 Coupé-USA/Japan (Manual/Auto)	1981	WPOJA092-BS820001 -	2500	1552/1529	95 x 78.9	4474
928S 4.7 Coupé (Manual/Automatic)	1981	WPOZZZ92ZBS840001 -	2500	1552/1529	97 x 78.9	4664
911 3.0 Coupé	1982	WPOZZZ91-CS100001 -	2272	1369/1379	95 x 70.4	2993
911 3.0 Targa	1982	WPOZZZ91-CS140001 -	2272	1372/1380	95 x 70.4	2993
930 Turbo 3.0 Coupé	1982	WPOZZZ93-CS000001 -	2272	1369/1379	97 x 74.4	3299
911-US 3.0 Coupé - USA	1982	WPOAA291-CS120001 -	2272	1369/1379	95 x 74.4	2993
911-US 3.0 Targa - USA	1982	WPOAA291-CS160001 -	2272	1372/1380	95 x 70.4	2993
930-CAN Turbo 3.3 Coupé - Canada	1982	WPOAA291-CS050001 -	2272	1369/1379	95 x 74.4	3299
911 3.0 Coupé - Japan	1982	WPOJA091-CS109500 -	2272	1369/1379	95 x 70.4	2993
911 3.0 Targa - Japan	1982	WPOJA091-CS149500 -	2272	1372/1380	95 x 70.4	2993
924 2.0 Coupé	1982	WPOZZZ92-CN400001 -	2400	1418/1372	86.5x 84.4	1984
924 Turbo 2.0 Coupé	1982	WPOZZZ93-CN100001 -	2400	1418/1372	86.5x 84.4	1984
924 2.0 Coupé - USA/Canada	1982	WPOAA292-CN450001 -	2400	1418/1372	86.5x 84.4	1984
924 Turbo 2.0 Coupé - USA/Canada	1982	WPOAA293-CN450001 -	2400	1418/1372	86.5x 84.4	1984
924 2.0 Coupé - Japan	1982	WPOJA093-CN400001 -	2400	1418/1372	86.5x 84.4	1984
924 Turbo 2.0 Coupé - Japan	1982	WPOJA093-CN100001 -	2400	1418/1372	86.5x 84.4	1984
928 4.7 Coupé	1982	WPOZZZ92-CS800001 -	2500	1552/1529	97 x 78.9	4664
928S 4.7 Coupé	1982	WPOZZZ92-CS840001 -	2500	1549/1521	97 x 78.9	4664

MODEL/TYPE	YEAR	FIRST VEHICLE IDENT NUMBER	WB-MM	TRACK F/R	BORE/STROKE	CC
928 4.7 Coupé - USA/Canada (Manual/Auto)	1982	WPOAA292-CS820001 -	2500	1552/1529	97 x 78.9	4664
928S 4.7 Coupé - Japan (Manual/Automatic)	1982	WPOZZZ92-CS809501 -	2500	1549/1521	97 x 78.9	4664
944 Coupé (Manual/Automatic)	1982	WPOZZZ94-CN400001 -	2400	1478/1476	100 x 78.9	2479
956 Twin-turbo-2.7 Competition Coupé	1982		2650	2000/2000	92.3 x 66	2649
911SC 3.2 Coupé	1983	WPOZZZ91-DS100001 -	2272	1372/1380	95 x 74.4	3164
911SC 3.2 Targa	1983	WPOZZZ91-DS140001 -	2272	1372/1380	95 x 74.4	3164
911SC 3.2 Cabriolet	1983	WPOZZZ91-DS150001 -	2272	1372/1380	95 x 74.4	3164
911 Turbo 3.3 Coupé	1983	WPOZZZ93-DS000001 -	2272	1432/1501	97 x 74.4	3299
911SC 3.2 Coupé - USA	1983	WPOAA291-DS120001 -	2272	1372/1380	95 x 74.4	3164
911SC 3.2 Targa - USA	1983	WPOAA291-DS160001 -	2272	1372/1380	95 x 74.4	3164
911SC 3.2 Cabriolet	1983	WPOAA291-DS170001 -	2272	1372/1380	95 x 74.4	3164
911 Turbo 3.3 Coupé - Canada	1983	WPOAA293-DS050001 -	2272	1432/1501	97 x 74.4	3299
911SC 3.2 Coupé - Japan	1983	WPOZZZ91-DS109501 -	2272	1372/1380	95 x 74.4	3164
911SC 3.2 Targa - Japan	1983	WPOZZZ91-DS149501 -	2272	1372/1380	95 x 74.4	3164
911SC 3.2 Cabriolet - Japan	1983	WPOZZZ91-DS159501 -	2272	1372/1380	95 x 74.4	3164
924 2.0 Coupé (Manual/Automatic)	1983	WPOZZZ92-DN400001 -	2400	1418/1372	86.5x 84.4	1984
924 Turbo 2.0 Coupé - Italy	1983	WPOZZZ92-DN100001 -	2400	1418/1372	86.5x 84.4	1984
928S 4.7 Coupé (Manual/Automatic)	1983	WPOZZZ92-DS840001 -	2500	1549/1521	97 x 78.9	4664
928S 4.7 Coupé - USA/Canada (Manual/Auto)	1983	WPOAA292-DS860001 -	2500	1549/1521	97 x 78.9	4664
928S 4.7 Coupé - Japan (Manual/Automatic)	1983	WPOZZZ92-DS849501 -	2500	1549/1521	97 x 78.9	4664
944 Coupé (Manual/Automatic)	.1983	WPOZZZ94-DN400001 -	2400	1478/1476	100 x 78.9	2479
944 Coupé - USA/Canada (Manual/Automatic)	1983	WPOAA294-DN450001 -	2400	1478/1476	100 x 78.9	2479
911 3.2 Carrera Coupé	1984	WPOZZZ01-ES100001 -	2272	1372/1380	95 x 74.4	3164
911 3.2 Turbo-Look Coupé	1984	WPOZZZ91-ES100001 -	2272	1432/1501	95 x 74.4	3164
911 3.2 Carrera Targa	1984	WPOZZZ91-ES140001 -	2272	1372/1380	95 x 74.4	3164
911 Turbo 3.3 Coupé	1984	WPOZZZ93-ES000001 -	2272	1432/1501	97 x 74.4	3299
911SC 3.2 Carrera Cabriolet	1984	WPOZZZ91-ES150001 -	2272	1372/1380	95 x 74.4	3164
911 3.2 Carrera Coupé - USA/Canada	1984	WPOAA291-ES120001 -	2272	1372/1380	95 x 74.4	3164
911 3.2 Turbo-Look Coupé - USA/Canada	1984	WPOAA291-ES120001 -	2272	1432/1501	95 x 74.4	3164
911 3.2 Carrera Targa - USA/Canada	1984	WPOAA291-ES160001 -	2272	1372/1380	95 x 74.4	3164
911SC 3.2 Carrera Cabriolet - USA/Canada	1984	WPOAA291-ES170001 -	2272	1372/1380	95 x 74.4	3164
911 Turbo 3.3 Coupé - Canada	1984	WPOAA293-ES050001 -	2272	1432/1501	97 x 74.4	3299
911 3.2 Carrera Coupé - Japan	1984	WPOZZZ91-ES109501 -	2272	1372/1380	95 x 74.4	3164
911 3.2 Turbo-Look Coupé - Japan	1984	WPOZZZ91-ES109501 -	2272	1432/1501	95 x 74.4	3164
911 3.2 Carrera Targa - Japan	1984	WPOZZZ91-ES149501 -	2272	1372/1380	95 x 74.4	3164
911SC 3.2 Carrera Cabriolet - Japan	1984	WPOZZZ91-ES159501 -	2272	1372/1380	95 x 74.4	3164
924 2.0 Coupé (Manual/Automatic)	1984	WPOZZZ92-EN400001 -	2400	1418/1372	86.5x 84.4	1984
924 2.0 Turbo Coupé - Italy	1984	WPOZZZ93-EN100001 -	2400	1418/1372	86.5x 84.4	1984
928S 4.7 Coupé (Manual/Automatic)	1984	WPOZZZ92-ES840001 -	2500	1549/1521	97 x 78.9	4664
928S 4.7 Coupé - USA/Canada (Manual/Auto)	1984	WPOAA292-ES860001 -	2500	1549/1521	97 x 78.9	4664
928S 4.7 Coupé - Japan (Manual/Automatic)	1984	WPOZZZ92-ES849501 -	2500	1549/1521	97 x 78.9	4664
944 Coupé (Manual/Automatic)	1984	WPOZZZ94-EN400001 -	2400	1478/1476	100 x 78.9	2479
944 Coupé - USA/Canada (Manual/Automatic)	1984	WPOAA294-EN450001 -	2400	1478/1476	100 x 78.9	2479
911 3.2 Carrera Coupé (also AUS/S/CH unlead)	1985	WPOZZZ91-FS100001 -	2272	1372/1380	95 x 74.4	3164
911 3.2 Carrera Targa (also AUS/S/CH unlead)	1985	WPOZZZ91-FS140001 -	2272	1372/1380	95 x 74.4	3164
911SC 3.2 Carrera Cabrio (& AUS/S/CH unlead)	1985	WPOZZZ91-FS150001 -	2272	1372/1380	95 x 74.4	3164
911 Turbo 3.3 Coupé	1985	WPOZZZ93-FS000001 -	2272	1432/1501	97 x 74.4	3299
911 3.2 Carrera Coupé - Switzerland	1985	WPOZZZ91-FS000001 -	2272	1372/1380	95 x 74.4	3164
911 3.2 Carrera Coupé - USA/Canada	1985	WPOAA291-FS120001 -	2272	1372/1380	95 x 74.4	3164
911 3.2 Carrera Targa - USA/Canada	1985	WPOAA291-FS160001 -	2272	1372/1380	95 x 74.4	3164
911SC 3.2 Carrera Cabriolet - USA/Canada	1985	WPOAA291-FS170001 -	2272	1372/1380	95 x 74.4	3164
911 Turbo 3.3 Coupé - Canada	1985	WPOAA293-FS050001 -	2272	1432/1501	97 x 70.4	3299
911 3.2 Carrera Coupé - Japan	1985	WPOZZZ91-FS109501 -	2272	1372/1380	95 x 74.4	3164
911 3.2 Carrera Targa - Japan	1985	WPOZZZ91-FS149501 -	2272	1372/1380	95 x 74.4	3164
911SC 3.2 Carrera Cabriolet - Japan	1985	WPOZZZ91-FS159501 -	2272	1372/1380	95 x 74.4	3164
924 2.0 Coupé (Manual/Automatic)	1985	WPOZZZ92-FN400001 -	2400	1418/1372	86.5x 84.4	1984
962 Twin-turbo 2.7 Competition Coupé	1985		2270	1665/1645	92.3 x 66	2649
928S 4.7 Coupé - (Manual/Automatic)	1985	WPOZZZ92-FS840001 -	2500	1549/1521	97 x 78.9	4664

MODEL/TYPE	YEAR	FIRST VEHICLE IDENT NUMBER	WB-MM	TRACK F/R	BORE/STROKE	CC
928S 4.7 Coupé - USA/Canada (Manual/Auto)	1985	WPOAA292-FS860001 -	2500	1549/1521	97 x 78.9	4664
928S 4.7 Coupé - Japan (Manual/Automatic)	1985	WPOZZZ92-FS849501 -	2500	1549/1521	97 x 78.9	4664
944 Coupé (Manual/Automatic)	1985	WPOZZZ94-FN400001 -	2400	1478/1476	100 x 78.9	2479
944 Coupé (Manual/Automatic)	1985	WPOZZZ94-FN420001 -	2400	1478/1476	100 x 78.9	2479
944 Coupé - USA/Canada (Manual/Automatic)	1985	WPOAA294-FN450001 -	2400	1478/1476	100 x 78.9	2479
944 Coupé - USA/Canada (Manual/Automatic)	1985	WPOAA294-FN470001 -	2400	1478/1476	100 x 78.9	2479
961 2.85 Twin-turbo Competition Coupé	1986		2310	1522/1580	95 x 67	2851
911 3.2 Carrera Coupé (incl AUS/CH/S)	1986	WPOZZZ91-GS100001 -	2272	1372/1380	95 x 74.4	3164
911 3.2 Carrera Targa (incl AUS/CH/S)	1986	WPOZZZ91-GS140001 -	2272	1372/1380	95 x 74.4	3164
911SC 3.2 Carrera Cabriolet (incl AUS/CH/S)	1986	WPOZZZ91-GS150001 -	2272	1372/1380	95 x 74.4	3164
911 Turbo 3.3 Coupé (incl CH version)	1986	WPOZZZ93-GS000001 -	2272	1432/1501	97 x 74.4	3299
911 3.2 Carrera Coupé - USA/Canada	1986	WPOAA291-GS120001 -	2272	1372/1380	95 x 74.4	3164
911 3.2 Carrera Targa - USA/Canada	1986	WPOAA291-GS160001 -	2272	1372/1380	95 x 74.4	3164
911SC 3.2 Carrera Cabriolet - USA/Canada	1986	WPOAA291-GS170001 -	2272	1372/1380	95 x 74.4	3164
911 Turbo 3.3 Coupé - USA/Canada	1986	WPOAA293-GS050001 -	2272	1432/1501	97 x 74.4	3299
924S 2.5 Coupé (Manual/Automatic)	1986	WPOZZZ92-GN400001 -	2400	1420/1393	100 x 78.9	2479
928S 4.7 Coupé (Manual/Automatic)	1986	WPOZZZ92-GS840001 -	2500	1549/1521	97 x 78.9	4664
928S 4.7 Coupé - USA/Canada (Manual/Auto)	1986	WPOAA292-GS860001 -	2500	1549/1521	97 x 78.9	4664
928S 4.7 Coupé - Japan (Manual/Automatic)	1986	WPOZZZ92-GS849501 -	2500	1549/1521	97 x 78.9	4664
944 Coupé (Manual/Automatic)	1986	WPOZZZ94-GN400001 -	2400	1478/1476	100 x 78.9	2479
944 Turbo Coupé	1986	WPOZZZ95-GN100001 -	2400	1477/1451	100 x 78.9	2479
944 Turbo Coupé	1986	WPOZZZ95-GN140001 -	2400	1477/1451	100 x 78.9	2479
944 Coupé - USA/Canada (Manual/Automatic)	1986	WPOAA294-GN450001 -	2400	1478/1476	100 x 78.9	2479
944 Turbo Coupé USA/Canada	1986	WPOAA295-GN150001 -	2400	1477/1451	100 x 78.9	2479
944 Coupé - Japan	1987	WPOZZZ94-GN400001 -	2400	1478/1476	100 x 78.9	2479
911 3.2 Carrera Coupé	1987	WPOZZZ91ZHS100001 -	2272	1372/1380	95 x 74.4	3164
911 3.2 Carrera Targa	1987	WPOZZZ91ZHS140001 -	2272	1372/1380	95 x 74.4	3164
911 3.2 Carrera Cabriolet	1987	WPOZZZ91ZHS150001 -	2272	1372/1380	95 x 74.4	3164
911 Turbo 3.3 Coupé	1987	WPOZZZ91ZHS000001 -	2272	1432/1501	97 x 74.4	3299
911 Turbo 3.3 Targa	1987	WPOZZZ91ZHS010001 -	2272	1432/1501	97 x 74.4	3299
911 Turbo 3.3 Cabriolet	1987	WPOZZZ91ZHS020001 -	2272	1432/1501	97 x 74.4	3299
911 3.2 Carrera Coupé - USA/Canada	1987	WPOAA291-HS120001 -	2272	1372/1380	95 x 74.4	3164
911 3.2 Carrera Targa - USA/Canada	1987	WPOAA291-HS160001 -	2272	1372/1380	95 x 74.4	3164
911 3.2 Carrera Cabriolet - USA/Canada	1987	WPOAA291-HS170001 -	2272	1372/1380	95 x 74.4	3164
911 Turbo 3.3 Coupé - USA/Canada	1987	WPOAA291-HS050001 -	2272	1432/1501	97 x 74.4	3299
911 Turbo 3.3 Targa - USA/Canada	1987	WPOAA291-HS060001 -	2272	1432/1501	97 x 74.4	3299
911 Turbo 3.3 Cabriolet - USA/Canada	1987	WPOAA291-HS070001 -	2272	1432/1501	97 x 74.4	3299
924S 2.5 Coupé (Manual/Automatic)	1987	WPOZZZ92ZHN400001 -	2400	1420/1393	100 x 78.9	2479
924S 2.5 Coupé USA/Canada (Manual/Automatic)	1987	WPOAA292-HN450001 -	2400	1420/1393	100 x 78.9	2479
928-S4 Coupé (Manual/Automatic)	1987	WPOZZZ92ZHS840001 -	2500	1551/1546	100 x 78.9	4957
928-S4 Coupé - Japan (Manual/Automatic)	1987	WPOZZZ92ZHS849501 -	2500	1551/1546	100 x 78.9	4957
928-S4 Coupé - USA/Canada (Manual/Automatic)	1987	WPOAA292-HS860001 -	2500	1551/1546	100 x 78.9	4957
944 Coupé (Manual/Automatic)	1987	WPOZZZ92ZHN420001 -	2400	1478/1476	100 x 78.9	2479
944S Coupé	1987	WPOZZZ94ZHN400001 -	2400	1478/1476	100 x 78.9	2479
944 Turbo Coupé	1987	WPOZZZ95ZHN100001 -	2400	1478/1476	100 x 78.9	2479
944 Coupé - USA/Canada (Manual/Automatic)	1987	WPOAA294-HN470001 -	2400	1478/1476	100 x 78.9	2479
944S Coupé - USA/Canada	1987	WPOAA294-HN450001 -	2400	1478/1476	100 x 78.9	2479
944 Turbo Coupé - USA	1987	WPOAA295-HN150001 -	2400	1477/1451	100 x 78.9	2479
944 Turbo Coupé - Canada	1987	WPOAA295-HN160001 -	2400	1477/1451	100 x 78.9	2479
959 2.85 Turbo Coupé	1987	WPOZZZ95-HS900001 -	2270	1505/1550	95 x 67	2851
911 3.2 Carrera Coupé	1988	WPOZZZ91ZJS100001 -	2272	1372/1380	95 x 74.4	3164
911 3.2 Carrera Targa	1988	WPOZZZ91ZJS140001 -	2272	1372/1380	95 x 74.4	3164
911 3.2 Carrera Coupé	1988	WPOZZZ91ZJS150001 -	2272	1372/1380	95 x 74.4	3164
911 Turbo 3.3 Coupé	1988	WPOZZZ91ZJS000001 -	2272	1432/1501	97 x 74.4	3299
911 Turbo 3.3 Targa	1988	WPOZZZ91ZJS010001 -	2272	1432/1501	97 x 74.4	3299
911 Turbo 3.3 Cabriolet	1988	WPOZZZ91ZJS020001 -	2272	1432/1501	97 x 74.4	3299
911 3.2 Carrera Coupé - Japan	1988	WPOZZZ91-JS109501 -	2272	1372/1380	95 x 74.4	3164
911 3.2 Carrera Targa - Japan	1988	WPOZZZ91-JS149501 -	2272	1372/1380	95 x 74.4	3164

MODEL/TYPE	YEAR	FIRST VEHICLE IDENT NUMBER	WB-MM	TRACK F/R	BORE/STROKE	CC
911 3.2 Carrera Coupé	1988	WPOZZZ91ZJS100001 -	2272	1372/1380	95 x 74.4	3164
911-CS (Club Sport) 3.2 Carrera Coupé	1988	WPOZZZ91ZJS105001 -	2272	1372/1380	95 x 74.4	3164
911 3.2 Carrera Targa	1988	WPOZZZ91ZJS140001 -	2272	1372/1380	95 x 74.4	3164
911 3.2 Carrera Cabriolet	1988	WPOZZZ91ZJS150001 -	2272	1372/1380	95 x 74.4	3164
911 Turbo 3.3 Coupé	1988	WPOZZZ91ZJS000001 -	2272	1432/1501	97 x 74.4	3299
911 Turbo 3.3 Targa	1988	WPOZZZ91ZJS010001 -	2272	1432/1501	97 x 74.4	3299
911 Turbo 3.3 Cabriolet	1988	WPOZZZ91ZJS020001 -	2272	1432/1501	97 x 74.4	3299
911 3.2 Carrera Coupé - Japan	1988	WPOZZZ91-JS109501 -	2272	1372/1380	95 x 74.4	3164
911 3.2 Carrera Targa - Japan	1988	WPOZZZ91-JS149501 -	2272	1372/1380	95 x 74.4	3164
911 3.2 Carrera Cabriolet - Japan	1988	WPOZZZ91-JS159501 -	2272	1372/1380	95 x 74.4	3164
924S 2.0 Coupé (Manual/Automatic)	1988	WPOZZZ92ZJN400001 -	2400	1420/1393	100 x 78.9	2479
924S 2.0 Coupé - USA/Canada (Manual/Auto)	1988	WPOAA292-JN450001 -	2400	1420/1393	100 x 78.9	2479
928-S4 Coupé (Manual/Automatic)	1988	WPOZZZ92ZJS840001 -	2500	1551/1546	100 x 78.9	4957
928-CS Coupé (Club Sport model)	1988	WPOZZZ92ZJS845001 -	2500	1551/1546	100 x 78.9	4957
928-S4 Coupé - Japan (Manual/Automatic)	1988	WPOZZZ92-JS849501 -	2500	1551/1546	100 x 78.9	4957
928-S4 Coupé - USA/Canada (Manual/Automatic)	1988	WPOAA292-JS860001 -	2500	1551/1546	100 x 78.9	4957
928-CS Coupé (Club Sport model) USA/Canada	1988	WPOAA292-JS865001 -	2500	1551/1546	100 x 78.9	4957
944 Coupé (Manual/Automatic)	1988	WPOZZZ94ZJN420001 -	2400	1478/1476	100 x 78.9	2479
944S Coupé	1988	WPOZZZ94ZJN400001 -	2400	1478/1476	100 x 78.9	2479
944 Turbo Coupé	1988	WPOZZZ95ZJN100001 -	2400	1477/1451	100 x 78.9	2479
944 Coupé - USA/Canada (Manual/Automatic)	1988	WPOAA294-JN470001 -	2400	1478/1476	100 x 78.9	2479
944S Coupé - USA/Canada	1988	WPOAA294-JN450001 -	2400	1478/1476	100 x 78.9	2479
944 Turbo Coupé - USA	1988	WPOAA295-JN150001 -	2400	1477/1451	100 x 78.9	2479
944 Turbo Coupé - Canada	1988	WPOAA295-JN160001 -	2400	1477/1451	100 x 78.9	2479
911 3.2 Coupé	1989	WPOZZZ91ZKS100001 -	2272	1372/1380	95 x 74.4	3164
911 3.2 Targa	1989	WPOZZZ91ZKS140001 -	2272	1372/1380	95 x 74.4	3164
911 3.2 Cabriolet	1989	WPOZZZ91ZKS150001 -	2272	1372/1380	95 x 74.4	3164
911 3.2 Coupé - USA	1989	WPOAB091ZKS120001 -	2272	1372/1380	95 x 74.4	3164
911 3.2 Targa - USA	1989	WPOEB091-KS160001 -	2272	1372/1380	95 x 74.4	3164
911 3.2 Cabriolet - USA	1989	WPOEB091-KS170001 -	2272	1372/1380	95 x 74.4	3164
911 Turbo 3.3 Coupé	1989	WPOZZZ93ZKS000001 -	2272	1432/1501	97 x 74.4	3299
911 Turbo 3.3 Targa	1989	WPOZZZ93ZKS010001 -	2272	1432/1501	97 x 74.4	3299
911 Turbo 3.3 Cabriolet	1989	WPOZZZ93ZKS020001 -	2272	1432/1501	97 x 74.4	3299
911 Turbo 3.3 Coupé - USA/Canada	1989	WPOJB093-KS050001 -	2272	1432/1501	97 x 74.4	3299
911 Turbo 3.3 Targa - USA/Canada	1989	WPOEB093-KS060001 -	2272	1432/1501	97 x 74.4	3299
911 Turbo 3.3 Cabriolet - USA/Canada	1989	WPOEB093-KS070001 -	2272	1432/1501	97 x 74.4	3299
928-S4/CS (Club Sport)/GT Coupés	1989	WPOZZZ92ZKS840001 -	2500	1551/1546	100 x 78.9	4957
928-S4/CS (Club Sport)/GT Coupés- USA/Canada	1989	WPOAA292-KS860001 -	2500	1551/1546	100 x 78.9	4957
944 Coupé (Manual/Automatic)	1989	WPOZZZ94ZKN400001 -	2400	1478/1476	100 x 78.9	2479
944 S2 Coupé	1989	WPOZZZ94ZKN400001 -	2400	1478/1476	104 x 88	2990
944 S2 Cabriolet	1989	WPOZZZ94ZKN430001 -	2400	1478/1476	104 x 88	2990
944 Turbo Coupé	1989	WPOZZZ95ZKN100001 -	2400	1477/1451	100 x 78.9	2479
944 Coupé - USA/Canada (Manual/Automatic)	1989	WPOAA294-KN450001 -	2400	1478/1476	100 x 78.9	2479
944 S2 Coupé - USA/Canada	1989	WPOAA294-KN450001 -	2400	1478/1476	104 x 88	2990
944 S2 Cabriolet - USA/Canada	1989	WPOAA294-KN480001 -	2400	1478/1476	104 x 88	2990
944 Turbo Coupé - USA/Canada	1989	WPOAA295-KN150001 -	2400	1477/1451	100 x 78.9	2479
911 3.6 Carrera 4 4WD Coupé (Man/Tiptronic)	1990	WPOZZZ96ZLS400001 -	2272	1380/1374	100 x 76.4	3600
911 3.6 Carrera 4 4WD Targa (Man/Tipt)	1990	WPOZZZ96ZLS410001 -	2272	1380/1374	100 x 76.4	3600
911 3.6 Carrera 4 4WD Cabriolet (Man/Tipt)	1990	WPOZZZ96ZLS420001 -	2272	1380/1374	100 x 76.4	3600
911 3.6 Carrera 2 Coupé (Manual/Tiptronic)	1990	WPOZZZ96ZLS400001 -	2272	1380/1374	100 x 76.4	3600
911 3.6 Carrera 2 Targa (Manual/Tiptronic)	1990	WPOZZZ96ZLS410001 -	2272	1380/1374	100 x 76.4	3600
911 3.6 Carrera 2 Cabrio (Manual/Tiptronic)	1990	WPOZZZ96ZLS420001 -	2272	1380/1374	100 x 76.4	3600
928-S4/GT Coupés	1990	WPOZZZ92ZLS840001 -	2500	1551/1546	100 x 78.9	4957
928-S4/GT Coupés - USA/Canada	1990	WPOAA292-LS860001 -	2500	1551/1546	100 x 78.9	4957
944 S2 Coupé	1990	WPOZZZ94ZLN400001 -	2400	1478/1476	104 x 88	2990
944 S2 Cabriolet	1990	WPOZZZ94ZLN430001 -	2400	1478/1476	104 x 88	2990
944 Turbo Coupé	1990	WPOZZZ95ZLN100001 -	2400	1478/1476	104 x 88	2990
944 S2 Coupé - USA/Canada	1990	WPOAA294-LN450001 -	2400	1478/1476	104 x 88	2990

MODEL/TYPE	YEAR	FIRST VEHICLE IDENT NUMBER	WB-MM	TRACK F/R	BORE/STROKE	CC
944 S2 Cabriolet - USA/Canada	1990	WPOAA294-LN480001 -	2400	1478/1476	104 x 88	2990
944 Turbo Coupé - USA/Canada	1990	WPOAA295-LN150001 -	2400	1478/1476	104 x 88	2990
911 3.6 Carrera 2 Coupé (Manual/Tiptronic)	1991	WPOZZZ96ZMS400001 -	2272	1380/1374	100 x 76.4	3600
911 3.6 Carrera 2 Targa (Manual/Tiptronic)	1991	WPOZZZ96ZMS430001 -	2272	1380/1374	100 x 76.4	3600
911 3.6 Carrera 2 Cabrio (Manual/Tiptronic)	1991	WPOZZZ96ZMS450001 -	2272	1380/1374	100 x 76.4	3600
911 3.6 Carrera 4 4WD Coupé (Man/Tiptr)	1991	WPOZZZ96ZMS400001 -	2272	1380/1374	100 x 76.4	3600
911 3.6 Carrera 4 4WD Targa (Man/Tiptr)	1991	WPOZZZ96ZMS430001 -	2272	1380/1374	100 x 76.4	3600
911 3.6 Carrera 4 4WD Cabrio (Man/Tiptr)	1991	WPOZZZ96ZMS450001 -	2272	1380/1374	100 x 76.4	3600
911 Turbo 3.3 Coupé	1991	WPOZZZ96ZMS470001 -	2272	1434/1493	97 x 74.4	3299
928-S4/GT Coupés	1991	WPOZZZ92ZMS800001 -	2500	1551/1546	100 x 78.9	4957
928-S4/GT Coupés	1991	WPOAA292-MS810001 -	2500	1551/1546	100 x 78.9	4957
944 S2 Coupé	1991	WPOZZZ94ZMN400001 -	2400	1478/1476	104 x 88	2990
944 S2 Cabriolet	1991	WPOZZZ94ZMN430001 -	2400	1478/1476	104 x 88	2990
944 Turbo Coupé	1991	WPOZZZ95ZMN100001 -	2400	1478/1476	104 x 88	2990
944 Turbo Cabriolet	1991	WPOZZZ95ZMN130001 -	2400	1478/1476	104 x 88	2990
944 S2 Coupé - USA/Canada	1991	WPOAA294-MN410001 -	2400	1478/1476	104 x 88	2990
944 S2 Cabriolet - USA/Canada	1991	WPOBA294-MN440001 -	2400	1478/1476	104 x 88	2990
911 3.6 Carrera RS Coupé	1992	WPOZZZ96ZNS490001 -	2272	1380/1374	100 x 76.4	3600
911 Turbo 3.3 Coupé	1992	WPOZZZ96ZNS470001 -	2272	1432/1501	97 x 74.4	3299
911 Turbo 3.3 Coupé - USA	1992	WPOAA296-NS480001 -	2272	1432/1501	97 x 74.4	3299
911 3.6 Carrera 2 & 4 (4WD) Coupé	1992	WPOZZZ96ZNS400001 -	2272	1380/1374	100 x 76.4	3600
911 3.6 Carrera 2 & 4 (4WD) Targa	1992	WPOZZZ96ZNS430001 -	2272	1380/1374	100 x 76.4	3600
911 3.6 Carrera 2 & 4 (4WD) Cabriolet	1992	WPOZZZ96ZNS450001 -	2272	1380/1374	100 x 76.4	3600
911 3.6 Carrera 2 & 4 (4WD) Coupé - USA/Can	1992	WPOAB296-NS420001 -	2272	1380/1374	100 x 76.4	3600
911 3.6 Carrera 2 & 4 (4WD) Targa - USA/Can	1992	WPOBB296-NS440001 -	2272	1380/1374	100 x 76.4	3600
911 3.6 Carrera 2 & 4 (4WD) Cabrio - USA/Can	1992	WPOCB296-NS460001 -	2272	1380/1374	100 x 76.4	3600
968 Coupé (Manual/Automatic)	1992	WPOZZZ96ZNS800001 -	2400	1478/1476	104 x 88	2990
968 Cabriolet (Manual/Automatic)	1992	WPOZZZ96ZNS830001 -	2400	1478/1476	104 x 88	2990
968 Coupé - USA/Canada (Manual/Automatic)	1992	WPOAB296-NS820001 -	2400	1478/1476	104 x 88	2990
968 Cabriolet - USA/Canada (Manual/Auto)	1992	WPOCB296-NS840001 -	2400	1478/1476	104 x 88	2990
928GTS 5.4 Coupé (Manual/Automatic)	1992	WPOZZZ92ZNS800001 -	2500	1551/1616	100 x 85.9	5397
928GTS 5.4 Coupé - USA/Canada (Manual/Auto)	1993	WPOAA292-PS815001 -	2500	1551/1616	100 x 85.9	5397

NB: Not all competition types are included in this Appendix after 1983.

Following the VIN numbering system:-

Many people find the VIN numbering system a total mystery. In fact, it is not difficult to follow once you understand that it consists of seventeen characters which are split into six groups, all of which have a particular meaning. Broken down, it looks like this:-

WPO ZZZ 91 ? PS1 00001

- 00001 — Serial Number of vehicle
- 1 — Last digit of Production Type Number (i.e: "4" of "944")
- S — Location of manufacturing plant (S = Stuttgart, N = Neckarsulm)
- P — Model Year (1992 = P)
- ? — Check digit (Porsche uses "Z" worldwide except USA/Canada, where it could be the digits "0 - 9" or the letter "X")
- 91 — First two digits of Production Type Number (i.e: "94" of "944")
- ZZZ — Spaces used in US to identify Body/Engine/Restraint system
- WPO — Manufacturer Code ("WPO" = Porsche)